# Education, T

## and

# Employment

### TOWARDS A NEW VOCATIONALISM?

The Open University

This reader is one part of an Open University integrated teaching system and the selection is therefore related to other material available to students. It is designed to evoke the critical understanding of students. Opinions expressed in it are not necessarily those of the course team or of the University.

# Education, Training
## and
# Employment

## TOWARDS A NEW VOCATIONALISM?

A Reader edited by

**ROGER DALE**

at the Open University

**PERGAMON PRESS**

OXFORD · NEW YORK · TORONTO · SYDNEY · FRANKFURT

in association with

**THE OPEN UNIVERSITY**

| U.K. | Pergamon Press Ltd., Headington Hill Hall, Oxford OX3 0BW, England |
| U.S.A. | Pergamon Press Inc., Maxwell House, Fairview Park, Elmsford, New York 10523, U.S.A. |
| CANADA | Pergamon Press Canada Ltd., Suite 104, 150 Consumers Road, Willowdale, Ontario M2J 1P9, Canada |
| AUSTRALIA | Pergamon Press (Aust.) Pty. Ltd., P.O. Box 544, Potts Point, N.S.W. 2011, Australia |
| FEDERAL REPUBLIC OF GERMANY | Pergamon Press GmbH, Hammerweg 6, D-6242 Kronberg-Taunus, Federal Republic of Germany |

Selection and editorial material
copyright © 1985 The Open University

First edition 1985

**Library of Congress Cataloging in Publication Data**
Main entry under title:
Education, training, and employment.
1. Industry and education—Great Britain—Addresses, essays,
lectures. 2. Youth—Employment—Great Britain—Addresses,
essays, lectures. 3. Vocational education—Great Britain—
Addresses, essays, lectures. I. Dale, Roger. II. Open
University.
LC1085.E3745   1985              370.19'3              85-9345

**British Library Cataloguing in Publication Data**
Education, training and employment: towards a new
vocationalism?
1. Education—Great Britain—Curricula
2. Vocational guidance—Great Britain
I. Dale, Roger
375'.0086'0941      LB027.5

ISBN 0-08-032673-0 Hardcover
ISBN 0-08-032672-2 Flexicover

*Printed in Great Britain by A. Wheaton & Co, Ltd., Exeter*

# Preface

This reader consists of a collection of articles which form part of the Open University Course E333, Policy-making in Education. The course critically examines way of analysing education policy, discusses the structure and process of educational policy-making in central and local government, and analyses educational policy in practice through case studies of particular policy issues.

The primary concerns of this reader are the policy responses to pressures to bring the education system into closer alignment with the priorities of employers, and to the problems created by very high levels of youth unemployment. Because the reader forms only one part of the course (much of which consists of written texts or broadcasts discussing issues raised in the reader articles), it cannot claim to offer a complete picture of educational policy-making. The selection of articles has been made with the overall course content in mind. It has been designed to highlight specific problems, and to develop the students' critical understanding. Opinions expressed within articles are, therefore, not necessarily those of the course team nor of the university. However, the editors believe that the selection, though not comprehensive, focuses on major issues in educational policy-making, and will be useful to anyone with an interest in the area.

There are three other readers, also published by Pergamon Press, and related to case studies of educational policy which we discussed in course material. These readers are:

*Policy-making in Education: the breakdown of consensus.* Edited by I. McNay and J. Ozga.

*Curriculum and Assessment: some policy issues.* Edited by P. Raggatt and G. Weiner.

*Race and Gender: equal opportunity policies in education.* Edited by M. Arnot.

It is not necessary to become an undergraduate of the Open University in order to study the course of which this reader is part. Further information about the course associated with this book may be obtained by writing to: The Admissions Office, The Open University, PO Box 48, Walton Hall, Milton Keynes MK7 6AB.

# Contents

# Introduction

It is almost a commonplace that the educational history of the past 150 years or so has been marked by continuing attempts to tie the education system more closely to the economy, to make schools serve the needs of industry more effectively.

All the contributions to this book address this problem more or less directly. What I want to do in this introduction is to provide a minimal context for those pieces by trying to unravel some of the many skeins that make up a complex web (for I would argue that they do not jointly form a coherent picture, and that much of the confusion surrounding the issue is rooted in the assumption that they must, somehow, form a clear picture), and make its effective resolution apparently so difficult. I shall suggest that the problem lies basically in simplification of both the educational attitudes, preferences and requirements of employers and of the available institutional provision, and in the consequent simplification of the attempts to bring the two together.

The first point to be made about employers' reactions to education, of course, is that they are not homogeneous. It is important to recognize, for instance, that very many jobs make no demands on schooling at all, but can be filled by people from quite different cultural backgrounds who may even speak no English. Apart from these jobs, there is no reason to suppose that the educational needs of large and small retailers, large and small manufacturers, garages, farmers and insurance brokers are all the same. Even within a single occupational area, say clerical work, educational requirements vary enormously. Further, it seems likely that all these different needs could be met simultaneously only with difficulty, and some of them may indeed be mutually incompatible. It should be borne in mind in the remainder of this introduction, then, that references to industry's or employers' needs, preferences or priorities for education cover a very wide range of differences.

It is a useful convenience to divide the aggregate of employers' reactions to the education system broadly into those emphasizing the knowledge, the skills and the attitudes which it is hoped that schools will promote in their pupils. (In this section of the introduction I am using 'schools' and 'education systems' interchangeably, since this undifferentiated conception of the possible institutional responses to industry's needs is rather typical of the

*1*

statements of such needs. The next section will break down that institutional provision, and there 'schools' will be used to distinguish one particular institutional response.)

In many ways, the issue of the appropriateness of the knowledge taught in the education system is the simplest of the three. It is this aspect of the gap between the economy and the schools which has received especially close scrutiny since the publication of Martin Weiner's *English Culture and the Decline of the Industrial Spirit*. Weiner's thesis is a simple one. From the middle of the nineteenth century a pseudo-aristocratic, 'gentrified' and anti-industrial culture has dominated the English bourgeoisie and created a climate inimical to industrial and economic development. The public schools and Oxford and Cambridge universities were key sites for the fostering of this culture, with their emphasis on the classics and disdain for technology and business. This attitude, it is alleged, has persisted and still permeates the education system. Each attempt to give greater emphasis to science and technology in schools, and to instal more practical, relevant curricula for them, has been countered by the process of 'academic drift', which ensures that values promoting education for its own sake continually edge out its more instrumental features. This process was continued in, and indeed led by, the universities (Scotland excepted), which encouraged their best products to carry out postgraduate work and pursue academic rather than industrial or business careers. As this point indicates, the 'Weiner thesis' has implications for attitudes as well as knowledge; the anti-industrial spirit is alleged to have infected teachers and led them to depreciate the importance, interest and rewards of careers in industry. It should be noted, though, that this critique is largely confined to the case of the more academic pupils and students.

The issue of skills is rather more complex. The major problem is that the whole concept is treated as though it were problematic. Of course, it is not. Its ideological nature is most readily apparent when we reflect how restricted to males the notion of skill is (see Wickham's paper in this volume). Skill is a political rather than a technical conception; as several writers (e.g. Sabel, 1981) have convincingly argued, skill is used to differentiate the work force for managerial purposes as much as to designate the capacity of individual workers. That industry has a pressing need for more skills is based on an opposite assumption, that the sum of *work* to be done is broken down into the skills people require, and the *jobs* they actually do in the most rational, technically efficient way; their content and specification being thus technically determined, it follows that the requirements of those to hold the jobs can be exactly determined in terms of skill, knowledge, etc. This false assumption goes at least some way to explaining another well-known problem concerning skills and qualifications—that the best qualified workers are by no means necessarily the most effective or productive workers (see Berg, 1970; Collins, 1979; Dale and Lemos Pires, 1984)—for if the concept of skill is not necessarily related to the performance of the job, it would be foolish to expect the most 'skilled' to be the most 'productive' workers.

This does not mean, of course, that *no* 'real' skill training is possible. It quite clearly is, and exactly how it should be done, and the precise allocation of responsibility for it between industry and schools, have also been matters of continuing discussion. The question is here less to do with the 'needs' of industry than with who should meet them.

Just as the 'knowledge' needs seem to relate especially to the most academic pupils, so the skills demands seem to have in mind the pupils of around average ability. And while, as suggested above, the attitudes towards productive work the education system instils into its pupils are frequently considered inappropriate right across the board, they are a particular concern currently in respect of the 'bottom 40 per cent'; as several of the articles below point out, inadequate knowledge of, and attitudes to, 'how the country makes its living' were a central theme of the Great Debate. That debate indeed crystallized what has been at the core of the issue of what should be the education system's and pupils' attitude towards industry. Essentially it was argued in the Great Debate and the Green Paper which followed it that schools should emphasize the contribution of the economy to national life and prepare pupils to take their place in that economy as it now exists. They should accept it and adapt to it as smoothly as possible. The alternative position in that debate, which at least implicitly informs much that teacher and educationist fear of, and opposition to 'vocational education' has still not been put more clearly than in the work of John Dewey. His approach is clear from the following.

> The kind of education in which I am interested is not one which will adapt workers to the existing industrial regime; I am not sufficiently in love with the regime for that. It seems to me that the business of all those who would not be educational time savers is to resist every move in this direction, and to strive for a kind of vocational education which will first alter the existing industrial system, and ultimately transform it (Dewey, 1977, p. 38).

## INSTITUTIONAL RESPONSES

Just as employers' needs of the education system are extremely varied, so too is the range of the system's response. I want here to isolate four institutional responses to those demands, schools and universities, further education, industrial training, and the careers service, and subsequently to consider the question—which runs right through this book—of how far those different institutional traditions and responses have been and are being brought together under the aegis of the Manpower Services Commission.

Most of the fire since the Great Debate and the Green Paper has been directed at the schools. They have been encouraged, cajoled, pressed, to make what they teach more relevant to knowledge, skills and attitudes and in tune with the current requirements of industry. That this pressure had been registered by the schools is clear from the following comment from two writers closely in touch with current developments in secondary education.

> In the past, the comprehensive school appeared to gear itself to meet its challenge from the pro-grammar school lobby, in terms of the performance of a minority of its pupils in the Ordinary and Advanced Certificates of Education. Now the emphasis is beginning to shift and schools are being questioned about their failure to equip their pupils with sufficient skills to adapt to current uncertainties attached to adult life (Galton and Moon, 1984, p. 5).

As Jamieson and I have both argued in our articles, the schools have not moved sufficiently far, or sufficiently rapidly, to fulfil the agenda laid down for them in the Green Paper to the satisfaction of their critics. The 'traditional bonds' between schools and industry have, as Watts points out below, become very stretched. There are a number of reasons for this: Watts discusses them at length and I have outlined some of them in my article. The reasons I give there emphasize the continuing, if diminishing, strength of schools' autonomy. What should be added here is that schools have always to some extent market-led, and have been influenced to a degree in their curriculum by the perceived vocational requirements of their pupils, and we might expect this kind of pressure to become more powerful as inter-school competition intensifies with falling rolls. This, of course, explains why schools have placed such an emphasis for so long on O and A level results; this emphasis is based not on ideological commitment as much as on recognition of necessity in the form of pupil and parent expectations.

The insulation of schools from industry, especially as the global term 'industry' becomes specified into local labour market requirements, has possibly then been overestimated. This point draws attention to two further points. First, it suggests some crucial differences in how schools relate to local labour markets. I have developed this point in my article below, but essentially there is a difference between preparing pupils to *get* jobs, which is what schools have always aimed to do, and preparing them, cognitively and attitudinally, to be better employees, which is what employers are in essence asking for. Second, it does suggest some recognition on the ground by employers, as mediated through their requirements of recruits, and potential recruits' requirements of schools, that there are limits both to schools' responsibility for the existing state of the economy and to their capacity to remedy it.

The second institutional response to be considered is the technical college/further education which is discussed in Gleeson's article (see also Parkes, 1985). This provision has traditionally been intimately linked to the requirements of local employers. As Reeder puts it, this sector 'has grown haphazardly, influenced by the availability of funds for capital expenditure, but dependent also on local and institutional aspirations' (1979, p. 136). This typified the sector even after attempts to expand and systematize the provision of technical training in the 1950s and 60s; many of these developments were associated with changes in the structure of industrial training. More recently the complex pattern of courses offered in what had been a locally based service have been put on a firm national footing with the creation of the Business and Technician Education Council. The courses of both sides of the partnership are, in different ways, highly vocational. As Avis puts it, 'the rhetoric and indeed the practice of skill training is intrinsic to TEC courses' (1981, p. 153), while he sees BEC courses as more centrally concerned with occupational socialization. Avis also quotes the chairman of the BEC as writing in his foreword to the Council's first policy statement in 1976 that BEC courses 'are basically vocational courses aimed at the needs of employers and students'; the foreword does go on, though, to deny that the courses are illiberal and insists that 'if they are taught properly they contain the basis of a sound broad education' (*ibid.*). That the chairman thought it necessary to defend the Council against a possible charge of illiberalism (and would it have been as necessary to do so nearly 10 years later?) reflects the fact that the FE sector too had been experiencing a form of academic drift, driven both by a proliferation of 'non-technical/vocational' courses and a feeling that they should provide an alternative source of post-16 general education to the schools. This is well caught in the following quotation.

Can we now convert, and transform that which has grown up as a means of 'instruction in technology', to a system of 'total education for a technological era?' For a rapidly increasing proportion of the population some form of technical, commercial and other vocational education provides their last contact with formal education; it must be, therefore, their 'finishing school' not only technically but educationally, giving them not only the 'means' of earning their living, but saying something also of the 'ends' to which that living should aspire (quoted in Leech, 1982, p. 23).

The most recent development in the FE sector has been, of course, the growth of what Gleeson calls '"the tertiary modern intake"', the unemployed and unemployable of the 1980's'. And with them has come MSC's highly significant ingress with its proposed takeover of 25 per cent of the sector, discussed at length in the articles by Gleeson, Farley and Finn.

The third institutional response is industrial training. As Anderson and Fairley (1983) point out, this is a complex area, with a range of policy implications not confined to the educational. Until relatively recent times, for instance, industrial training was dominated by, and could almost be equated with, apprenticeship, a means of controlling the flow of labour as well as a form of skill training.

Prior to the Industrial Training Act of 1964, industrial training had been carried out by employers on a voluntary basis, with state intervention confined to the local technical colleges which, as stated above, were frequently direct providers to industry of the skill training that was done. This voluntary system was held, however, to be producing a shortage of skilled labour. The 1964 Act was designed to remedy this. As Anderson and Fairley put it, 'The major justification for the form of intervention represented by the Act was the widespread desire to generalize from existing "best practice" in training and to do so through structures which would leave employers with a direct stake in the training system which would facilitate the constant development of training practice to meet changing industrial needs' (1983, pp. 194–5). All firms in the industry were subject to a training levy which made the system both funded by and responsible to industry, though changes in training policy and practice had to be agreed by both sides of the industry.

Farley's paper in this volume goes into the reasons for the growing disaffection with the ITB system of training that led to its effective supersession in the 1973 Act, which brought the MSC into the picture for the first time. It is interesting and perhaps significant that the MSC entered the area of education–economy links through the particular form of institutional response in which state educational and training provision (in the form of FE) was most directly shaped by the local, and increasingly after 1964 the national, needs of industry.

The fourth and final form of institutional response to be mentioned, the careers service, commonly receives little attention in this context, perhaps because it is seen by both the education system and industry as somehow an adjunct of the other. Indeed, as Showler points out, the 'conflict in views about whether the Youth Employment Service is primarily an educational or an employment service responsibility has been a feature of discussion and legislation concerning the service throughout its history' (1976, p. 64). It changed its name to the Careers Service only after the Education and Training Act of 1973, when it was given a functional remit to deal with students in schools and further and higher education, rather than be concerned with the employment problems of the whole particular age group. Throughout its recent history, however, as Showler shows, its emphasis has been much more on the vocational guidance, rather than the industrial placement, side of its activities. It has provided a service to young people by informing them about work and especially by making them aware of their own capacities, rather than to industry by finding suitable recruits.

Of these four modes of institutional response, then, only one, industrial training, places an unambiguous priority on meeting the needs of industry rather than meeting the needs of the individual. All the rest have been subject, to a greater or lesser degree, to a drift from 'training' to 'education', from employers' preferences and priorities, to students' right to a full realization of their potential as the key organizing principle. Though the two are not necessarily mutually incompatible—and indeed the possibility that the comprehensive school would serve both purposes better than the tripartite system was a quite central part of the argument which brought it into being—the tension between them has been a continuing feature of aspects of social and industrial policy as well as of educational policy in this country.

To conclude this introduction I want to suggest that a central theme, more or less prominent in all the papers in this volume, is the possibility that we are now witnessing the beginnings of a concerted and comprehensive attempt to resolve that tension, drawing together the four existing forms of institutional responses. The views of the authors vary both as to the strength of this possibility and to its desirability, but there is a measure of agreement about its organizational basis, the MSC, and its broad ideology, which has been called the new vocationalism.

I will not, therefore, elaborate on them here, but will make four more general points in conclusion. First, the boundaries of the new vocationalism are clear—it is intended for the 14–18-year-old age group, and aimed much more at the lower two-thirds of the ability range than at those who are able to follow the traditional academic route. Second its broad aims are clear—and they differ somewhat from those typically found in education–employment discussions due to the shadow of extremely high levels of youth unemployment and the possibility that they may be permanent. The aims are not confined to training young people for jobs, but also include the need to adjust them to a new status, somewhere between work and non-work. The objectives of the new vocationalism are as much occupational versatility and personal adjustment as anything that would formerly have been recognized as skill training. Third, it appears to have done little to overcome the existing limitations in respect of the opportunities available to girls and ethnic minorities. And finally, in spite of its wide range of support at the highest levels, and however strong or weak it may be, the new vocationalism itself does not go unresisted or unimpeded by the interests and ideologies which have continually reasserted the values of education.

## REFERENCES

Anderson, Malcolm, and Fairley, John (1983) The politics of industrial training in the United Kingdom. *Journal of Public Policy*, **3**, 2, 191–208.

Avis, James (1981) Social and technical relations: the case of further education. *British Journal of Sociology of Education*, **2**, 2, 145–61.

Berg, Ivar (1970) *The Great Training Robbery*, Praeger, New York.

Collins, Randall (1979) *The Credential Society*, Academic Press, New York and London.

Dale, Roger, and Lemos Pires, Eurico (1984) Linking people and jobs: the indeterminate place of educational credentials, in Broadfoot, P. (ed.), *Selection, Certification and Control*, Falmer Press, Lewes, pp. 51–65.

Dewey, J. (1977) Education vs. trade training: Dr Dewey's reply. *Curriculum Inquiry*, **7**, 37–39.

Galton, Maurice and Moon, Bob (eds.) (1984) *Changing Schools . . . Changing Curriculum*, Harper and Row, London.

Leech, Michael (1982) The college and its environment, in Parkes, D. (ed.), *The Changing Face of Further Education*, FEU, London, pp. 23–26.

Parkes, David (1985) Competition . . . and competence? Education, teaching and the roles of DES and MSC, in McNay, I. and Ozga, J. (eds.), *Policy-making in Education: the breakdown of consensus*, Pergamon Press, Oxford.

Reeder, David (1979) A recurring debate: education and industry, in Bernbaum, G. (ed.), *Schooling in Decline*, Macmillan, London, pp. 115–48.

Sabel, Charles F. (1981) *Politics and Work: the Division of Labour in Industry*, Cambridge University Press, Cambridge.

Showler, Brian (1976) *The Public Employment Service*, Longman, London.

---

# 1

---

# Education and Employment
## the traditional bonds

### A.G. WATTS

Education has, of course, much loftier ideals than those of preparation for employment. At its best, it is concerned with the development of the individual's full range of abilities and aptitudes, with the cultivation of spiritual and moral values, with the nurturing of imagination and sensibility, with the transmission and reinterpretation of culture. Indeed, there is a strong tradition within education which derides the instrumental or utilitarian, and which regards vocational matters as being improper educational concerns. As Peterson (1975) puts it:

> Education is, by tradition and in theory, a leisure activity. The word school is etymologically associated with leisure and the belief that 'study' and 'scholarship' and 'learning' should be undertaken for their own sake and arise from the individual pupil's interest is a cliché of the educational theorist and of the prize-giving address (p. 93).

Nonetheless, education has a close relationship with the world of work. Societies expect schools to develop in young people the knowledge, attitudes and skills which will enable them to contribute to the economy. Young people and their parents, too, expect schools to help them enter a worthwhile job. In a survey carried out by Morton-Williams and Finch (1968), 87 per cent of 15-year-old school-leavers thought that schools should 'teach you things which will help you to get as good a job or career as possible' (pp. 33–34) and 89 per cent of parents agreed with them (p. 39). Only 47 per cent of teachers and 28 per cent of heads at that time considered this objective as very important for schools (p. 42). Teachers frequently, however, find it useful to invoke the claim 'If you work hard, you will get a good job'.

Historically, the vocational connections of education in Britain are strong

*Source:* From Watts, A.G. (1983) *Education, Unemployment and the Future of Work*, Open University Press, Milton Keynes.

and pervasive. As Williams (1961) points out, the first English schools, from the late sixth century, had a primarily vocational intention: that of training intending priests and monks to conduct and understand the services of the Church, and to read the Bible and the writings of the Christian Fathers (pp. 127–8). As education grew during the Middle Ages, it 'was organized in general relation to a firm structure of inherited and destined status and condition: the craft apprentices, the future knights, the future clerisy' (p. 131). This remained true through to the eighteenth century, which was remarkable for the growth of a number of new vocational academies, serving commerce, engineering, the arts, and the armed services (p. 134): in these academies, young people were prepared for the occupation they were to assume and the place in society it implied. The old classical education was still focused towards the old professions for which it had a vocational appropriateness—the church, the law (and later, as it grew, towards the Civil Service).

It was only really during the Industrial Revolution that, as Williams puts it, 'the old humanists muddled the issue by claiming a fundamental distinction between their traditional learning and that of the new disciplines'—notably science and technical education:

> ... it was from this kind of thinking that there developed the absurd defensive reaction that all real learning was undertaken without thought of practical advantage. In fact, as the educational history shows, the classical linguistic disciplines were primarily vocational, but these particular vocations had acquired a separate traditional dignity, which was refused to vocations now of equal human relevance (p. 142).

The result was that élite educational institutions from the Victorian era tended to propagate a particular academic and cultural heritage which was associated with a gentlemanly disdain for vocational application, and particularly for industrial manufacture. The seductive social advantages attached to these strategies helped to produce a 'gentrification of the industrialist', which—it has been influentially argued—has contributed significantly to Britain's economic decline (Wiener, 1981).

At the same time, however, the Industrial Revolution also saw the gradual extension of schooling from select and usually privileged groups to the mass of the population. Again, vocational motives were present. The new factories required large numbers of skilled and semi-skilled employees. Workers recruited for the land were notoriously ill-adapted to factory disciplines, and the schools were seen as one way in which they could be socialized into such disciplines. The aim was explicitly expressed by William Temple, when advocating in 1770 that poor children should be sent at the age of four to workhouses where they should be employed in manufactures and given two hours' schooling a day:

> There is considerable use in their being, somehow or other, constantly employed at least twelve hours a day, whether they earn their living or not; for by these means, we hope that the rising generations will be so habituated to constant employment that it would at length prove agreeable and entertaining to them ... (quoted in Thompson, 1967, p. 84).

Factories required time-discipline, they required obedience, and they required a capacity to engage in rote, repetitive work. The new elementary schools were structured to develop all three, as well as to develop the basic skills of reading and counting that would equip workers to understand and implement simple instructions.

During the nineteenth century, such schooling was extended to all. In 1816 about 58 per cent of children attended a school of some kind for some period; by 1835 the figure had risen to 83 per cent, though the average duration of school attendance was still only one year; by 1851 the average duration had been raised to two years; and in 1870 universal elementary schooling became compulsory (Williams, 1961, pp. 136–7). The notion of compulsory schooling owed much to the 'public educators', who argued that men had a natural right to be educated, and that any good society depended on governments accepting this principle as their duty (*ibid.*, p. 141). It also owed much to those who argued that a limited education in appropriate attitudes and habits—diligence, thrift, sobriety, deference to superiors, etc.—was necessary for social and political stability (see Simon, 1960, chapter III). On the whole, it was the links between the concerns of the latter group and the focus of the 'industrial trainers' on the social character required by the industrial work-place which tended to be predominant in determining the content of the elementary school curriculum. They were even more influential on the method of pedagogy, with its emphasis on formal instruction requiring pupils to perform specified tasks within set periods of time determined by their teachers.

The battle between the 'public educators', the 'industrial trainers' and the 'old humanists'—as Williams (*ibid.*) terms them—continued through the nineteenth and into the twentieth centuries. Gradually, scientific and technical education became established in the schools and universities, though still subject to the snobberies of the 'old humanists'. Gradually, too, the school-leaving age was raised, partly in response to arguments about the upgrading of the skill requirements of jobs and the need for the country to utilize more fully its human resources and talents. In 1944 secondary education for all was established on a tripartite basis—grammar, technical, and secondary modern. The divisions were intended to be broadly related to likely occupational destinations. Technical schools, designed largely to prepare for technician-level occupations, were never established on any very extensive scale; the grammar schools, however, led clearly to 'white-collar' occupations, while the secondary modern led to 'blue-collar' occupations (Swift, 1973). The tripartite structure accordingly produced a system of what Turner (1960) termed 'sponsored' mobility, in which students were selected early for their occupational and social level, and thereafter were prepared for this status in terms partly of appropriate skills, but also of appropriate expectations, standards of behaviour, and values.

The rigidities of this system attracted increasing criticism during the 1950s and 1960s. It was pointed out that early selection meant decisions about the level of pupils' occupational destinations were being made prematurely before their abilities and aptitudes were evident, and that this had the effect of reinforcing the advantages stemming from their home background (Floud *et al.*, 1956). The ideological concern for greater equality of opportunity, together with the demands for a more highly skilled work-force from a then prospering economy, provided a climate in which the decision was made to merge the three forms of school into comprehensive schools catering for the full range of ability. The system of 'sponsored' mobility was accordingly replaced to some extent by a system of 'contest' mobility. This Turner (1960) likened to a race or other sporting event, in which all compete on equal terms for a limited number of prizes, and in which premature judgements on the results of the race are avoided.

In the event, this change was never fully implemented. Some areas continued to maintain selective schooling, in practice and even sometimes in name. The differences between catchment areas meant that comprehensive schools in some areas were very like grammar schools, whereas in others they were virtually indistinguishable from secondary moderns. Again, the retention of rigid streaming in many comprehensive schools permitted curricular divisions to survive institutional integration. Finally, the continued existence of élite forms of education outside the state educational system, in the independent schools, meant that some parents continued to be able to purchase advantageous positions in the 'race'.

The incomplete implementation of the comprehensive school reforms meant that the socialization processes within schools preparing pupils for their levels of occupational destination continued to operate (Ashton and Field, 1976), but that they were increasingly concealed within a curriculum structure and examination system which permitted all pupils to take part in the 'race' instead of prematurely excluding large numbers from it. Whereas in 1961/2 73 per cent of pupils in England and Wales had left school without even attempting a public school-leaving examination (Ministry of Education, 1964, table B), the growth of comprehensive schools—along with the advent of the CSE, and the raising of the school-leaving age to 16—meant that by 1973/4 only 20 per cent of pupils left school in England without a graded GCE/CSE result, and by 1980/1 this figure had fallen to 11 per cent (DES, 1982b, table 3). Since the main prizes were perceived as being associated with 'white-collar' work, almost all pupils became subjected to a more academic curriculum, with increased emphasis on the acquisition of knowledge and the ability to reproduce it on paper for the benefit of examination assessors (Dore, 1976). While the content of the curriculum thus became less relevant to the occupations which many pupils would come to perform, its connections with the world of employment grew no less. Its basic rationale was that it provided a meritocratic foundation on which selection for occupational destinations could be based. If secondary schools in particular no longer *prepared* pupils for particular forms of employment in such an overt and direct way as hitherto, what they did continued to be influenced and justified by the extent to which it determined *access* to employment.

## THE BONDS

It will be evident from this brief historical outline that links with employment have been, and continue to be, a powerful influence on the development of education in Britain. In broad terms, four functions which educational institutions can play in relation to employment can be distinguished: those of selection, socialization, orientation, and preparation. Each will now be briefly examined in turn.

(1) *Selection.* Over the past century or so, there has been a steady movement from the ascription of status by birth to the achievement of status through education. As a result, the educational process has ceased to be concerned simply with the transmission of skills and values: increasingly it has taken on the functions of allocating and selecting as well as training individuals for their adult roles (Banks, 1976, p. 5). Particular educational qualifications are now necessary prerequisites for entry to many occupations, and are used in selection by many employers. The case for credentialism of this kind is partly based on a utilitarian principle of *efficiency,* recognizing the importance of developing the society's talents to the full and deploying them to maximum effect, so that the most able people can find their way into the most important and demanding jobs. In part, too, it is concerned with *equity,* making it possible for the social status of individuals to be determined by their talents and their efforts rather than by the accidents of birth.

It is important to recognize that in practice credentialism seems to satisfy neither of these principles very satisfactorily. In terms of efficiency, the relationship between educational qualifications and degree of success in an occupation is often very low (for American evidence on this, see Hoyt, 1965; Collins, 1979, pp. 19–20). This may be partly because professional associations, in the search for reduced supply and increased status, are constantly upgrading the educational qualifications required for entry (Dore, 1976, pp. 24–28; Watts, 1973b); the same process is used by employers seeking convenient ways of restricting the number of job applicants to a manageable size. As Berg (1970) has shown in the United States, this process of meritocratic inflation can proceed to a point where, far from adding to workers' productivity and satisfaction, it reduces them because the workers are over-qualified and their skills are not being utilized. Moreover, many of the attributes which are most important in determining occupational success—social skills, for example—are not measured by educational qualifications. Such qualifications are thus often used as criteria for occupational entry not because they are relevant but because they are administratively convenient and publicly defensible.

Their defensibility is largely due to the appearance they give of being socially equitable. But here, too, there is room for scepticism. Bourdieu and Passeron (1977) argue that schools trade in exclusive forms of 'cultural capital' based on the symbols, language forms, structure and meanings of bourgeois culture, and that students with access to such cultural capital—primarily through their families—do well in school because educational achievement is measured in terms of the skills and the knowledge which the cultural capital provides. Certainly it is the case that upper-middle-class children born in the period 1930–49 were three times as likely as lower-middle-class children to reach a university, and nearly 12 times as likely as lower-working-class children to do so (Halsey, 1975, p. 14). Admittedly these differentials were lower than for children born during the period 1910–29, suggesting some reduction of social class inequalities of access to educational opportunities. Westergaard and Resler (1975, pp. 324.6), however, have suggested that this moderate widening of education as an avenue of ability has been counteracted by a concomitant contraction of other channels of mobility—notably independent entrepreneurial activity and mid-career promotion up the rungs of bureaucratic hierarchies—resulting from, among other things, increased attention to educational qualifications in schools and colleges. As a result, they argue, credentialism and the expansion of educational provision are likely to have had little or no net impact on social mobility. Even if one does not argue such an extreme case, it is clear that credentialism does not remove inequalities, and that even if it diminishes them to some extent, it adds apparent legitimacy to those that remain.

Moreover, the extent of the use made of educational qualifications should not be exaggerated. As Maguire and Ashton (1981) demonstrate, employers do not in practice place such emphasis on educational qualifications as schools often imagine they do. At the higher levels of the occupational hierarchy, qualifications are often necessary but not sufficient: employers use them as a convenient pre-selection device when deciding which applicants to consider more closely, but thereafter pay little attention to them. At the lower occupational levels, qualifications are frequently used simply as crude measures not of cognitive abilities but of such normative qualities as perseverance and capacity for hard work, or are ignored altogether.

Nonetheless, the process of credentialism has had a powerful effect on education. It has increased the demand for education; it has also affected its nature. In surveys conducted in Ireland, Raven (1977) found that the goals to which primacy was attached by pupils, ex-pupils, parents, teachers and employers—for example, the fostering of personal qualities and capabilities like initiative, self-confidence, and the ability to deal with others—received scant attention in schools and, as a result, were poorly attained. Teachers and pupils worked not towards the goals which they believed to be the most important from an educational point of view, but towards goals that could be assessed in a manner acceptable for the award of educational qualifications. The result was to restrict what went on in schools to activities that were narrowly utilitarian and instrumental in scope. The available evidence indicates that much the same is true in Britain.

This process contains many ironic contradictions. Intrinsic educational values are subordinated to the extrinsic need to provide tickets to employment. Yet the content of these 'tickets' has very little direct vocational relevance, and its indirect relevance is much more pertinent to white-collar than to other occupations. The content is controlled not by employers but, ultimately, by the universities. For at each stage of the educational system, the content of the curriculum tends to be determined by the needs not of those who will 'drop out' at that stage, but of those who will go on to the next; and at the apex of this structure stand the universities, which in addition exert a powerful influence on school examination boards. Their control 'protects' the school curriculum from vocational influence, in line with the heritage of Williams' 'old humanists'. The status of subjects tends to be measured by the extent to which they have moved away from utilitarian or pedagogic traditions and have become 'academic' (Goodson, 1983).

The result is an extension to almost all school pupils of an academic curriculum very like that previously offered only to the few in the grammar schools. This curriculum is experienced by many young people as irrelevant to their immediate and future interests. The notion that the traditional liberal curriculum has some particular intrinsic virtue which work-oriented subjects do not, as a medium through which spiritual, intellectual and aesthetic powers can be developed, is itself open to question (Peterson, 1975, p. 95). But even if it were true, the chances of achieving these ends with pupils suspicious of such a curriculum are greatly diminished by the examination system, which means that these pupils see the curriculum chiefly as a means of labelling them as failures through an opaque process based on restricted academic criteria. They are aware that the applicability of these criteria outside the educational world is highly disputable, particularly in the non-professional and non-clerical jobs for which many of them are destined. Moreover, although the whole process is justified to them by the supposed need to perform a sorting and preselection function for employers, this service in reality is not as widely used by employers as is commonly supposed; and because of their limited vantage point, pupils tend to underestimate even the extent to which it is used (see Gray *et al.*, 1983, pp. 136–41).

Thus although the examination system provides an effective motivational spur for some, it is counter-productive for others, and can indeed alienate them permanently from formal learning. It also more generally develops an instrumental attitude to learning and work in which intrinsic motives such as actual enjoyment of working hard are rejected and regarded as socially unacceptable (Turner, 1983). Indeed, Flude and Parrott (1979, pp. 67–68) consider that 'it is the attitudes and values engendered by public examinations, and the image of education which this adolescent, academic steeplechase provokes in parents, teachers and pupils, which represent the main barrier to the development of recurrent education'.

(2) *Socialization.* The second function which educational institutions can play in relation to employment is that of influencing students' attitudes to the world of work, and to their own function within it, through the formal and informal organization of educational institutions and the social relations within them. In the United States, Bowles and Gintis (1976) have argued that in many key respects the structure and social relations of education accurately reflect and reproduce the structure and social relations of the work-place. Both are organized hierarchically; in both, alienated workers are motivated by extrinsic rewards (examination marks in school, pay at work); and in both, work tasks are fragmented. This 'close correspondence between the social relationships which govern personal interaction in the work place and the social relationships of the educational system' (*ibid.*, p. 12) means that schools nurture, within young people of different types, attitudes and behaviour consonant with their likely future levels of participation in the labour force. Those destined for managerial and professional occupations are presented during their educational careers with situations in which they are asked to be autonomous, independent and creative; those destined for the shop-floor are subjected to custodial regimes which stress obedience to rules, passivity and conformity.

In the British context, Ashton and Field (1976) have described how the identities of pupils destined for different occupational levels are established or reinforced by the identities created within their schools. Thus those destined for 'extended careers'—characterized by long training and the continuing prospect of advancement—come to see themselves as possessing superior abilities, to see the successful performance of their allotted school tasks in the light of the long-term rewards associated with the entry into a 'good career', and to understand the importance both of personal advancement and of loyalty to the organization. The importance of 'getting on' and of 'making something of themselves' is also transmitted to those destined for 'short-term careers'—in skilled manual trades, technical occupations, and some forms of clerical and secretarial work—which again are characterized by formal training but which offer little chance of advancement beyond a certain level. Here, though, the organizational structure of the school, including streaming and more informal channelling mechanisms, restricts their access to the certification required for entry to extended careers.

Finally, those destined for 'careerless occupations'—which require little training and offer no prospects of promotion and little or no intrinsic job satisfaction—receive derogatory messages which, as we have seen, teach them to see themselves as 'failures'. Their realization that academic subjects have no rewards to offer them persuades them instead to seek some alternative sources of reward or satisfaction in the here and now—for example, through persistent rule-breaking and 'messing about'. Not only are these young people committed to semi-skilled and unskilled work by their educational experience, but their self-image of being academically inferior, their concern with obtaining extrinsic rewards as immediately as they can, and their desire to leave school as soon as possible, all mean that jobs of this kind have certain attractions. As Willis (1977) points out, this means that the very forms of resistance used within a school counter-culture by alienated groups of working-class boys lead them to make a largely willing entry into unskilled forms of labour, in which they are subsequently trapped—a powerful, even poignant, form of 'self-induction'. They even presage the forms of resistance—skiving etc.—which will enable them to cope with the monotony of such jobs.

Such analyses can evidently be applied too rigidly, to a point where they become mechanistic and deterministic. Clearly there are many respects in which schools do not reproduce the values and social relations of the workplace. Indeed, some influential commentators in recent years have argued that schools do not mirror the world of work well enough, but instead encourage patterns of dependency and immaturity which inhibit the process of transition to adulthood and to employment (Bazalgette, 1978a; Scharff, 1976). Clearly, too, the divisions between the groups distinguished by Ashton and Field are not as rigidly marked as the description above might suggest. The movement from a 'sponsored' to a 'contest' system—however incomplete it may have been—means that the forces of socialization have been weakened somewhat, because the point of differentiation has been postponed, and its rigidity relaxed to some extent. Teachers have become more resistant to the notion that they should be performing a 'sorting' function, and adapting pupils to accept low-level jobs which make little use of their potential. Such resistance has indeed proceeded to a point where numbers of employers have grown concerned about the discrepancies between the expectations and attitudes that school-leavers have been encouraged to develop and the demands that will realistically be made of them (for a useful analysis of these and other differences of view between teachers and employers, see Bridges, 1981). Nonetheless, the changes that have taken place in opening up opportunities within educational institutions are often more apparent than real: for example, secondary school pupils continue to be sifted by teachers in terms of their perceived aptitudes, despite the rhetoric of pupils making their own subject 'choices' (Woods, 1979, especially chapter 2). The process of socialization into employment remains a strong feature of the educational system—all the stronger because it is often implicit rather than explicit, and hidden even to the teachers who promote it.

(3) *Orientation.* The third function is concerned with deliberate curricular interventions designed to help students to understand the world of employment, and to prepare for the choices and transitions they will have to

make on entering it. To some extent it can be seen as an attempt to reinforce the process of socialization where it is not proving sufficiently effective. Alternatively, it can also be seen as being designed to make the process more visible and therefore open to questions and deliberation—to make it a learning process rather than merely a conditioning process.

This orientation function has two distinguishable facets. One is *careers education*, which is concerned with helping students to prepare for their individual career choices and transitions. From its traditionally peripheral position within education, based on narrow concepts of information-giving and individual interviewing, careers guidance in the early 1970s increasingly came to be incorporated into the curriculum itself (Schools Council, 1972; DES, 1973; Watts, 1973a). Many schools and other educational institutions now have curricular programmes focused around four broad aims: 'opportunity awareness', covering awareness of the range of alternatives open in and around the world of work, the demands they make, and the rewards and satisfactions they offer; 'self awareness', covering awareness of the distinct abilities, interest, values, etc., that define the kind of person one is and/or wishes to become; 'decision learning', covering development of decision-making skills; and 'transition learning', covering development of skills to cope with the transition to work and subsequent career transitions (Law and Watts, 1977). Some schools establish careers education as a separate 'subject'; some integrate it into a broader programme of social and personal education; and some seek to 'infuse' it across the traditional areas of the curriculum. A survey conducted in 1975-8 by Her Majesty's Inspectorate (DES, 1979a, p. 230) found that half of secondary schools had a programme of this kind in the fourth and fifth years for all their pupils, and a further 12-15 per cent a programme for some of their pupils. Careers-education programmes have also been introduced in higher education (Watts, 1977b) and for adults (Watts, 1980). The notion that careers-education programmes can help people to participate actively in the decisions that determine their lives has been questioned by Roberts (1977, 1981), who argues that in reality people's lives are largely determined by the opportunity structure, and that many people have to accept what they can get. This has been disputed by other writers (e.g. Daws, 1977, 1981; Law, 1981a, 1981b), who have argued that there remains sufficient scope for such programmes to have an impact.

The second facet of the orientation function is *learning about work*, as part of social and political education within (in particular) schools. The central concept here is that all school pupils—regardless of when and where they are to work themselves, and as part of the preparation for their role not of *worker* but of *citizen*—should be taught to understand the place of work in society. Various approaches have been developed, including curriculum courses on 'industry' and related topics, and infusion of such topics into traditional subjects across the curriculum. There has also been emphasis on experiential methods, including work experience, work simulation, and the use of 'adults other than teachers' (including employers and trade unionists) in the classroom (see Jamieson and Lightfoot, 1982; Watts, 1983a).

A particular concern behind many such programmes has been the notion that young people should understand the process of wealth generation in general and the role of manufacturing industry in particular. Discussion of such matters is in principle welcomed not only by the political right but also by the left, so long as it is possible to regard the *status quo* as open to challenge and question (see e.g. Edgley, 1977). In practice, however, the boundaries set by government statements and the like tend to be narrow, and to avoid any suggestions that the matters under discussion are disputable or politically controversial. Some teachers thus fear that if they engage in such issues, they will be compelled to engage in a form of indoctrination. Accordingly, they sometimes prefer to evade the issues altogether (Beck, 1981, p. 89). Significantly, the most effective project in this area—the Schools Council Industry Project—has disarmed such suspicions by having the support of the Trades Union Congress as well as the Confederation of British Industry, and has adopted a low-profile approach in which emphasis has been placed not on centrally-produced policy statements and curriculum materials, but on encouraging local curriculum development which is experience-based and in which the teachers' role is shared to a much greater extent than is usual with employers, unionists and other members of the community (see Jamieson and Lightfoot, 1982).

(4) *Preparation.* The fourth and final function is that of promoting the acquisition of specific skills and knowledge which students will be able to apply in a direct way after entering employment. As we have seen, this function was strongly evident in the practice of education up to the Industrial Revolution, if only in relation to certain occupations. Subsequently it has diminished in prominence, certainly within schools and universities. The general view has come to be that such preparation should properly be left to employers and to other post-school institutions like colleges of further education and polytechnics. It is argued, for example, that introducing significant vocational training into schools would require resources, equipment and expertise which schools rarely possess. It would also run the danger of limiting pupils' occupational horizons prematurely, and—unless great care was taken—it might develop knowledge and skills which would be inappropriate to, or would rapidly become outdated in, a changing labour market. Further, it is pointed out that many of the skills that are most important at work are generic skills like numeracy and literacy: if schools concentrate on these, then they are providing a form of preparation but without closing options unnecessarily.

On the other hand, it is recognized that what the Brunton Report in Scotland felicitously termed the 'vocational impulse' (SED, 1963, p. 24) can be a powerful incentive to learning. Also, unless steps are taken to introduce a wider range of vocational skills into the school curriculum, the effects of schooling may be to establish a bias in favour of the white-collar occupations to which, as was suggested earlier, the academic forms of learning used in schools tend to be most relevant. The result may be to raise aspirations which cannot be met, and to develop attitudes that impede occupational flexibility.

On the whole, however, the tendency until recently has been to limit the extent to which schools have been involved in vocational preparation. The vocational courses set up in many secondary-modern schools in the 1950s to yield the motivational advantages of the 'vocational impulse' largely disappeared with comprehensive reorganization, and teachers became resistant to them, for reasons already mentioned. Even employers tended on the whole to bear out the findings of the Carr Committee (National Joint Advisory Council, 1958, p. 23) that 'the overwhelming majority of industries are of the opinion that education given at school before the minimum school-leaving age is reached should be general rather than vocational in character' and should not engage in offering 'some sort of vocational instruction which industry itself is much better qualified to give'. Trade unions, too, consistently opposed vocational education in schools, on the grounds that it would operate to the disadvantage of working-class children, who would be bound to be pressurized into forms of work which were more appropriate to their social station than to their innate aptitudes and abilities (Jamieson and Lightfoot, 1982, p. 39). Certainly the evidence from such programmes in the United States indicates that, narrowly defined, they are almost invariably limited to low-attaining students and lower-level occupations, that they restrict access to higher-status and better-paid jobs, and that they accordingly acquire a stigma which limits and in time discredits their appeal (Grubb and Lazerson, 1981). In short, the irony of vocational-preparation programmes is that they tend to deprive their students of access to what in terms of status and income must be regarded as the *real* vocational prizes.

## REFERENCES

Ashton, D.N. and Field, D. (1976) *Young Workers*, Hutchinson, London.
Banks, O. (1976) *The Sociology of Education* (3rd edition), Batsford, London.
Bazalgette, J. (1978) *School Life and Work Life*, Hutchinson, London.
Beck, J. (1981) Education, industry and the needs of the economy, *Cambridge Journal of Education*, 2, 2.
Berg, I (1970) *The Great Training Robbery*, Penguin, Harmondsworth.
Bourdieu, P. and Passeron, J.C. (1977) *Reproduction in Education, Society and Culture*, Sage, London.
Bowles, S. and Gintis, H. (1976) *Schooling in Capitalist America*, Routledge & Kegan Paul, London.
Bridges, D. (1981) Teachers and the 'World of Work', in Elliot, J., Bridges, D., Ebbutt, D., Gibson, R. and Nias, J. (eds.), *School Accountability*, Grant McIntyre, London.
Collins, R. (1979) *The Credential Society*, Academic Press, New York.
Daws, P.P. (1977) Are careers education programmes in schools a waste of time?—a reply to Roberts, *British Journal of Guidance and Counselling*, 5, 1.

Daws, P.P. (1981) The socialization/opportunity—structures theory of the occupational location of school leavers: a critical appraisal, in Watts, A.G., Super, D.E. and Kidd, J.M. (eds.), *Career Development in Britain*, CRAC/Hobson, Cambridge.

Department of Education and Science (1973) *Careers Education in Secondary Schools, Education Survey 18*, HMSO, London.

Department of Education and Science (1979) *Aspects of Secondary Education in England*, a survey by HM Inspectors of Schools, HMSO, London.

Department of Education and Science (1982) *Department 17+: a New Qualification*, HMSO, London.

Dore, R. (1976) *The Diploma Disease*, Allen & Unwin, London.

Edgley, R. (1977) Education for industry, *Educational Research*, **20**, 1.

Floud, J., Halsey, A.H. and Martin, F.M. (1956) *Social Class and Educational Opportunity*, Heinemann, London.

Flude, R. and Parrott, A. (1979) *Education and the Challenge of Change*, Open University Press, Milton Keynes.

Goodson, I.F. (1983) *School Subjects and Curriculum Change*, Croom Helm, London.

Gray, J., McPherson, A.F. and Raffe, D. (1983) *Reconstruction of Secondary Education*, Routledge & Kegan Paul, London.

Grubb, W.N. and Lazerson, M. (1981) Vocational solutions to youth problems: the persistent frustrations of the American experience, *Educational Analysis*, **3**, 2.

Halsey, A.H. (1975) Sociology and the equality debate, *Oxford Review of Education*, **1**, 1.

Hoyt, D.P. (1965) The relationship between college grades and adult achievement: a review of the literature, Iowa City: American College Testing Program, Iowa City.

Jamieson, I. and Lightfoot, M. (1982) *Schools and Industry*, Methuen, London.

Law, B. (1981a) Careers theory: a third dimension?, in Watts, A.G., Super, D.E. and Kidd, J.M. (eds.), *Career Development in Britain*, CRAC/Hobsons, Cambridge.

Law, B. (1981b) Community interaction: a 'mid-range' focus for theories of career development in young adults, *British Journal of Guidance and Counselling*, **9**, 2, July.

Law, B. and Watts, A.G. (1977) *Schools, Careers and Community*, Church Information Office, London.

Maguire, M.J. and Ashton, D.N. (1981) Employers' perceptions and use of educational qualifications, *Educational Analysis*, 3, 2.

Ministry of Education (1984) *Statistics of Education (1962), Part Three*, HMSO, London.

Morton-Williams, R. and Finch, S. (1968) *Young School Leavers*, Schools Council Enquiry One, HMSO, London.

National Joint Advisory Council (1958) *Training for Skill* (Carr Report), HMSO, London.

Peterson, A.D.C. (1975) Education for work or for leisure?, in Haworth, J.T. and Smith, M.A. (eds.), *Work and Leisure*, Lepus, London.

Raven, J. (1977) *Education, Values and Society*, Lewis, London.

Roberts, K. (1977) The social conditions, consequences and limitations of careers guidance, *British Journal of Guidance and Counselling*, **5**, 1, January.

Roberts, K. (1981) The sociology of work entry and occupational choice, in Watts, A.G., Super, D.E. and Kidd, J.M. (eds.), *Career Development in Britain*, CRAC/Hobsons, Cambridge.

Scharff, D.E. (1976) Aspects of the transition from school to work, in Hill, J.M.M. and Scarff, D.E. (eds.), *Between Two Worlds*, Careers Consultants, London.

Schools Council (1972) *Careers Education in the 1970s*, Working Paper 40, Evans/Methuen, London.

Scottish Education Department (1963) *From School to Further Education* (Brunton Report), HMSO, Edinburgh.

Simon, B. (1960) *Studies in the History of Education 1780–1870*, Lawrence & Wishart, London.

Swift, B. (1973) Job orientations and the transition from school to work: a longitudinal study, *British Journal of Guidance and Counselling*, **1**, 1.

Thompson, E.P. (1967) Time, work-discipline and industrial capitalism, *Past and Present*, No. 38.

Turner, G. (1983) *The Social World of the Comprehensive School*, Croom Helm, London.

Turner, R.H. (1960) Sponsored and contest mobility and the school system, *American Sociological Review*, **25**, 5.

Watts, A.G. (1973a) A structure for careers education, in Jackson, R. (ed.), *Careers Guidance; Practice and Problems*, Arnold, London.

Watts, A.G. (1973b) The qualifications spiral, *Sunday Times Magazine*, 7 October.
Watts, A.G. (1977) A policy for youth?, *The Ditchley Journal*, **4**, 1, Spring.
Watts, A.G. (1980) Educational and careers guidance services for adults: II. A review of current provision, *British Journal of Guidance and Counselling*, **8**, 2.
Watts, A.G. (1983) (ed.) *Work Experience and Schools*, Heinemann, London.
Westergaard, J. and Resler, H. (1975) *Class in a Capitalist Society*, Heinemann, London.
Weiner, M.J. (1981) *English culture and decline of the industrial spirit, 1850-1980*, Cambridge University Press, Cambridge.
Williams, R. (1961) *The Long Revolution*, Chatto & Windus, London.
Willis, P. (1977) *Learning to Labour*, Saxon House, Farnborough.
Woods, P. (1979) *The Divided School*, Routledge & Kegan Paul, London.

# 2

# Corporate Hegemony or Pedagogic Liberation?

## the schools-industry movement in England and Wales

IAN JAMIESON

## INTRODUCTION

It has probably always been the case that employers operating in a market economy are dissatisfied in one way or another with the performance of their employees. The reasons for this go beyond the scope of this essay, but are related to such factors as the difficulties in assessing the work capacity of individual workers at the time of selection (cf. the purchase of machinery), and the difficulties inherent in the employers' attempts to harness the talents and capacities of autonomous human beings for their own ends.

In seeking to account for the poor, or at least variable, performance of their workers, employers seek scapegoats. If we took the population of workers in general, then the list of potential scapegoats is very long. We would soon be into such popular territory as 'national culture' and other 'explanations' that have been made so popular by writers like Weiner (1981). If we narrowed our scope, however, and concentrated on young workers—first time entrants to employment—then the explanations become altogether firmer.

School-leavers are an important part of the labour force. Over 57 per cent of 1983/84 16-year-olds were available for work, some 1.6 million young people. For the majority of employers this is the largest group of employees that they take on in any one year. Not only are they the largest group of

Specially commissioned for this volume.
© The Open University, 1985.

employees for many employers, but they traditionally make less 'good employees' than other groups. There are many reasons for this: their position in the life cycle gives them fewer responsibilities and cares compared with other workers; their set of 'working skills', both technical and social, tend to be less well developed than other employees; they are still at the stage of establishing some sort of 'fit' between their identity as individuals and the demands of particular occupations and/or employers. These factors, which have always been present, produce a characteristic pattern of young worker behaviour. This is marked by frequent job changes (unless prevented by very high unemployment rates), and by noticeably higher absenteeism, accident and lateness records. In short, such workers are, in employers' terms, less responsible than many other groups of employees.

Although we have argued that there are certain characteristic features of the work performance of young people that are endemic to this form of labour, employers are rarely either brought into contact with such arguments, or impressed with them when they do encounter them. Employers react in a number of different ways to the 'problem'. Some try to substitute other forms of labour which they believe to be more pliant and reliable, for example married women workers. When the labour market allows it, some employers expend more effort on the selection process in order to try to make sure that their employees are of better quality than those of their competitors.

One feature of the school-leaver labour market which many employers observe, and which appears to damage the analysis of the 'young worker syndrome' that we have outlined above, is the fact that the 'problem' seems to vary over time. Sometimes the cohort of school-leavers appears better adapted to the world of work than others. There are a number of quite straightforward explanations of this phenomenon. In the first place it is true that the quality of 16-year-olds available for work has declined over the recent past. This is because more and more able students have either stayed on at school, or have gone on to further or higher education. Employers who have stuck with recruiting this age group are thus recruiting from a significantly different range of ability. Our second explanation, by contrast, produces a rise in the quality of recruits. The slackening in the demand for all labour from the early 1970s has meant that the pool of workers from which employers can choose has grown. This has allowed employers to become more selective about their young recruits and to choose those who appear to have mastered certain basic skills, and who have an appropriate set of 'attitudes'.


## LET'S BLAME EDUCATION

We have spent some time analysing the problems that employers have with young workers, because it is this phenomenon that is at the heart of the schools-industry movement. As we shall show, the movement that was reborn in the 1970s is composed of a wide variety of different groups, organized in different ways and with different goals and interests, but we must never forget that it is primarily driven by the recruitment problems of employers.

Of course employers recognize that their young worker problems are unlikely to be fundamental to the success of the business, although such 'soft' factors as the general attitude or culture of the work force might be (cf. Peters and Waterman, 1982). Poor economic performance at either the level of the firm or the economy must entail a consideration of a wider set of factors. It is important to realize this fact because the schools-industry movement that arose from the ashes of previous similar movements must also be placed in the context of the wider debate about the performance of the British economy.

The British economy has been declining steadily since its heyday in the 1850s. At each new turn in the crisis the debate about the causes of the decline has intensified. The social fabric of the society has been earnestly scrutinized in an attempt to see which elements of it were not congruent with the needs of the economy. The fortunes of education have varied. In the late 1950s and 1960s there was a view that 'in a modern economy the quality and efficiency of the working population very largely depend on the educational system' (Floud, 1961). The restructuring of schools along comprehensive lines was begun, at least partly, because it was believed that such a system would make better use of the 'pool of ability', and thus ultimately benefit the economy.

In the 1970s the faith in education as a contributor to economic well-being quickly ebbed away. The oil crisis of 1973/4 helped to usher in a new economic analysis that saw education, alongside other state services, as part of a policy of social engineering that was syphoning off wealth from the economic heart of the society. It was at this time that the macroeconomic analysis of economists and politicians of the political right was brought together with the microanalysis of employers. Together they erected the ideological stage on which that great show, the Great Debate, could be performed.

The employers focused on their problems with young employees. Although several social institutions were implicated in the problem, for example family life and the mass media, it was the schools that were directly in the firing line. After all weren't the schools directly responsible for the fact that 'children these days couldn't add up and spell?' and weren't employers justified in expecting the schools to educate for employment?—after all they were paying for them via taxation and rates. These local cries of anguish contributed significantly to the growing mood of disillusionment with education. The Black Papers[1] had attempted to give a veneer of respectability to the view that

---

[1] The Black Papers were five papers published between 1969 and 1977 that attacked aspects of what they called 'progressive' or 'socially motivated' developments in the educational system (see Cox and Dyson, 1969).

standards were falling. Some economists argued that education was assisting in the shift of resources away from the wealth-creating private manufacturing sector towards the non-productive service sector (Bacon and Eltis, 1976). This was happening both because of the enormous cost of the education system, and because teachers were not encouraging able young people to go into industry as a career, particularly manufacturing industry. All this presaged a scrutiny of the great secret garden of education—the curriculum.

## THE GREAT DEBATE

The Great Debate—a public dialogue about the system of education in England and Wales—was formally opened by the then Prime Minister, James Callaghan, at a speech at Ruskin College, Oxford in 1976. One of the major themes of the speech, and of the series of regional conferences that were subsequently held, was the lack of relationship between industry and education. It should be clear from the foregoing analysis that the Ruskin speech did not conjure up the schools-industry debate out of thin air; rather it gave a focus and added legitimacy to many existing complaints about the education system.

The charges that Callaghan levelled against the education system were ones with which many people, both inside and outside education, had some sympathy. Indeed several organizations and projects had been launched before the Ruskin speech in order to try and remedy some of the alleged deficiencies. These included the Schools Council Industry Project—a tripartite CBI/TUC/Schools Council venture; Understanding British Industry—a CBI initiative; Project Trident—an organization dedicated to widening the experiences of young people, especially in the work area; the Standing Conference on School Science and Technology and many more. The Great Debate was not a tightly focused challenge to the education system; it contained a myriad of elements. It could be described in much the same way as political journalists are apt to describe Chancellors' budgets—there was something in it for everybody.

## THE SCHOOLS-INDUSTRY MOVEMENT IN THE
## 1980s

It is difficult to describe the schools-industry movement. There are two major difficulties. First, it doesn't stand still. The number of groups, organizations and government agencies constantly grows. Secondly, it has no one focus of attention, save that it wants to change the education system in one way or another. The agenda of the movement changes with the vicissitudes of the economy, and as emphasis and money are placed on different facets. Like many other movements dependent on financial donations from government and industry, it is subject to fashion and political whim. In summary, the movement can be described as a diverse collection of employer and trade union groupings; specially constructed educational or quasi-educational 'projects'; government agencies and government statements and exhortations—all designed to put pressure on the education system to change the content of what is taught, how it is taught, and how it is assessed and examined. Its focus is largely on secondary education, and within that primarily on the 14–19 age group.

## SKILLS, ATTITUDES AND KNOWLEDGE

Although the schools-industry movement is difficult to describe, it is possible to provide a crude analytical map of some of its major interests by delineating some of the skills, attitudes and knowledge that it tries to promote inside the school system.

Of the three elements the skills component is the most difficult to describe. This is because many of the things described as skills by the schools-industry lobby are not skills at all, but either attitudes or knowledge. The second difficulty is that it is in this area that the greatest shifts of emphasis have taken place.

In the beginning there were 'basic skills'. Basic skills meant literacy (later extended to communication skills) and numeracy. The main protagonists of basic skills were local employers who claimed in the mid 1970s that their school-leaver recruits couldn't add up or spell. This lobby received powerful support from the Black Paper movement.

Numeracy and literacy weren't the only problems of employers. Their complaints were soon extended to encompass the 'fact' that school-leavers were poor at being interviewed; listening to and following instructions; social and interpersonal skills at the workplace—in short, a wide range of skills which it was alleged every competent adult needed at the workplace. This rather heterogeneous collection of skills soon came to be dubbed 'social and life skills'.

The other strand of the skills component is more difficult to grasp. Its roots lie in the relatively low status accorded to the 'practical' professions in England and Wales—particularly engineering. When this is extended to schools it becomes a concern that teachers unconsciously, or sometimes even consciously, dissuade young people from considering careers in technological occupations. The scope for studying technological subjects at school, particularly for girls, is generally assessed as poor. One outcome of this state of affairs is a shortage of technicians and technologists, particularly in the electronics field, one of the few industrial sectors to hold up during the economic depression. Employers have seized on this shortage as yet more evidence of the shortcomings of the education system.

Yet the malaise is thought to be wider than mere technological inadequacy in the schools. It is that our schools are not producing young people who are 'practically capable' in the modern world. Significantly, it is argued, we even have difficulty in expressing the deficiency, and adherents of this view fall back on the French word *métier* or the German *technik*. In England it finds its expression in the Education for Capability movement. This alliance of educationalists and industrialists wishes to make 'knowing how' at least as important as 'knowing that' in the school system.

If skills are not the traditional fare of the school curriculum, then attitudes have an even less legitimate place, at least in the formal curriculum. Of course most teachers are aware that schools are one institutional part of the process of attitude formation amongst young people, but they are apt to shift the blame for dysfunctional attitudes on to those other powerful socializing agencies, the family and the mass media.

In many ways the 'attitude problem' is regarded by many members of the schools-industry movement as the key problem. This is certainly true for the employer community. At the end of the day most employers believe that they can remedy deficiencies in basic skills amongst their new recruits, and they can train youngsters in technical skills. These are only issues for employers because they believe that the schools should be doing a better job in these two respects. The attitude of young people towards work, employment, the reward structure of industry—even the system of private enterprise itself—gives them much more cause for concern.

Attitude change is a sensitive issue for most teachers. Whereas the inculcation of knowledge or skills is regarded as legitimate, attitudes lie in a dangerous border region. Over that border lies the infamous land of propaganda. Is this the reason why much of the concern about the attitudes of young people towards work is obfuscated by referring to them as skills? A cynic might indeed be tempted to conclude that the emphasis on social and life skills is no more than a modern version of the nineteenth-century worry about the attitudes of the labouring classes, and might be confirmed in this view on discovering that in practice the only young people who receive such training are those destined for working class jobs, or unemployment (Atkinson *et al.*, 1982).

The traditional curriculum arena for schools in England and Wales is not skills or attitudes, it is knowledge. Whilst it is generally accepted that there is a distinction between knowledge and skills (between knowing that, and knowing how—although the distinction is not nearly so clear cut as most imagine), many in the schools-industry field have a naive view about the relationship between knowledge and attitudes. At its most simplistic, it is the view that if only the children knew and understood some basic facts about the industrial world then their attitudes would change. Such a view is held as strongly in the trade union movement, which is worried about young people's attitude towards the trade unions as well as their reluctance to join, as it is amongst employers, who are worried about their view of industrial careers, and of the nature of industrial and commercial life. Both groups have good cause for concern (Jamieson and Lightfoot, 1982).

The knowledge strand of the schools-industry movement takes many forms. Curiously, it informs much of the experience-based learning that is characteristic of schools-industry work, i.e. the practice that places many young people in real or realistic work situations. Such a practice emanates from the belief, in both industry and the trade unions, not only that they are misunderstood by school students, but that if those students came into greater contact with 'real' industrialists and trade unionists, then they would form a more favourable view. Such a position is perfectly legitimate if somewhat optimistic (cf. Jamieson and Lightfoot, 1982).

A more traditional view is that much of the problem stems from a fundamental misunderstanding of some basic facts of economic life. This line is perhaps most clearly articulated by Sir Keith Joseph, the Secretary of State for Education, who in a written parliamentary answer, subsequently sent to all Chief Education Officers in England and Wales, declared that,

> Schools and businesses need to understand each other better. Business should be helped to appreciate the aims of the schools and the context in which these seek to achieve them. Conversely, schools and pupils need to be helped to understand how the nation earns its living in the world. This involves helping pupils to understand how industry and commerce are organised; the relationship of producers and consumers; the process of wealth creation; the role played by choice, competition and profit; and the traditional liberal view of the interdependence of political and economic freedom, as well as rival theories of how production and distribution should be organised and the moral basis commonly adduced by those theories (Joseph, 1982).

Thus, if pupils understand the process of wealth creation then it is believed that more would be attracted to careers in industry and commerce, particularly the more able, and would be better motivated to work.

## THE ANALYSIS OF CHANGE

The analysis that we have offered of the schools-industry movement, describing it by reference to the skills, attitudes and knowledge which it wishes to promote in schools, shows something of the diversity of the movement. That diversity is also a function of the large number of different organizations and pressure groups trying to bring about change in the school system.

The process of educational change in England and Wales is often a great puzzle to foreign observers. The problem is that whilst we have a national system of education it is organized locally, and the Local Education Authorities and their schools have enormous discretion. Indeed, in terms of the curriculum the discretion is almost total. The most important consequence of the devolved system of organization is that for change to take place it becomes necessary to convince education authorities and the schools of the need for change. It is also necessary to point out that there is no mechanism which automatically adjusts the education system to the 'needs of the economy' or to the needs of employers, even supposing it was clear what the needs of the economy were, or that employers spoke clearly and with one voice about their own requirements.

To describe the agencies of change operating in the schools-industry field is then to describe the organization of pressure on schools exerted by outside organizations. We can identify three main areas of pressure on the schools. The first comes from central government; the second from local employers; the third from ad hoc projects and organizations specifically designed to change some elements of schooling.

The main arm of central government that deals with the school system is the Department of Education and Science. The DES has issued a stream of documents urging LEAs and their schools to draw closer to industry and to make their curricula more relevant to the needs of industry and commerce. The Department was responsible for the Education (Work Experience) Act, 1973. This important piece of enabling legislation opened the doors to work experience for school pupils, a central schools-industry activity. The Inspectorate (HMI) have also devoted considerable time and energy to schools-industry matters. They have offered specific advice to schools within their general curriculum documents, and they have published case studies of practice (HMI, 1981). The HMI have also urged teacher-training establishments to include 'preparation for working life' in their pre-service courses (HMI, 1982).

The DES and Her Majesty's Inspectors of Schools have not however, been the most influential arm of government in schools-industry matters. This is because their stock in trade is advice and exhortation, a commodity in considerable oversupply in the schools system. By contrast, money is a commodity that is conspicuously short in the system and it is by their control of such a resource that two other arms of government, the Department of Trade and Industry (DTI) and the Manpower Services Commission (MSC), have become important agencies for change. The DTI has from its budget of £2 million per year (excluding the microelectronics programme) financed important developments in school science and technology, but most significantly has helped LEAs set up local change agents—the network of Schools-Industry Liaison Officers (SILOS). The MSC launched a five-year major curriculum programme in 1983, the Technical and Vocational Education Initiative (TVEI), at an annual cost of over £25 million. The SILO programme is discussed in more detail later in this essay, and TVEI is the subject of Dale's article in this volume.

The second source of pressure on schools is employers. In terms of their importance for schools, it is *local* employers that are significant. They are significant in two ways. First, they can exert pressure on the schools just because they are local. As businessmen or councillors they may sit on the governing body of schools; as parents they can exert pressure through the PTA or other similar bodies. As significant members of the local community they have access to the local media—in the middle seventies many local papers carried employer broadsides against schools for not achieving basic levels of competence amongst their pupils. The second source of local business influence resides in their role as local employers of labour. Most young people who leave school at 16 and get a job find employment locally. Local employers are thus the direct recipients of the schools' output. Discrimination against the products of one school, or public denunciation of a particular school's ability in a certain curriculum area, can therefore be particularly powerful.

Also on the local stage are employer groupings like local chambers of commerce, or organizations like Rotary which are largely composed of business people. These often act as facilitating agencies when schools wish to arrange something which involves employers, but they rarely act as pressure groups.

One or two organizations and some very large companies are active on the national stage. Firms like BP, Unilever, and ICI; organizations like the CBI and TUC; the Bank Information Service, the Engineering Industry Training Board and several others, are prominent at this level. These organizations play several important roles in schools-industry work. In the first place they provide individuals to sit on the wide range of committees, project-steering groups, and advisory panels that preside over various schools-industry activities. Secondly, they try to energize their local 'branches' to participate actively in local schools-industry matters. Finally, the commercial organizations channel significant funds into the schools-industry movement, largely but not solely, through the established schools-industry projects like Trident, Understanding British Industry, Understanding Industry and, to a lesser extent, the Schools Council Industry Project.

The last source of pressure on the schools comes from a curiously British educational phenomenon—the project. Because each school is more or less allowed to decide its own curriculum, then curriculum change comes about by what often amounts to a sales campaign mounted by various agencies.

Schools-industry work in England and Wales is marked by the existence of a large number of national and local projects all trying to persuade schools to change some existing practice, or adopt a new programme. The unpublished Cooper Report commissioned by the DES to chart the area found fourteen major projects working in the nation's schools, and innumerable local endeavours. These national projects were spending £2.9 million annually (1981 prices).

The majority of these projects are single purpose projects, in business to try to persuade schools to adopt one particular educational programme or idea. Some of the best known projects include Project Trident, whose major activity is to organize work experience for pupils; Young Enterprise, which arranges for students to set up their own business enterprises; Understanding Industry, which arranges for industrialists to give talks to schoolchildren. There are two large multi-purpose organizations whose remit is much wider. Understanding British Industry (UBI) is a CBI project whose activities include in-service training for teachers and general help and advice for LEAs. The largest organization is the School Curriculum Industry Project, formerly the Schools Council Industry Project (SCIP). An LEA has to formally join this organization, whose aim is to promote curriculum development in the schools-industry field. Over half of the LEAs in England and Wales belong to SCIP. It is distinctive in at least two respects: (1) it is the only organization whose money comes out of public funds, all the rest competing for funds from private industry; (2) it is the only organization formally supported by the TUC, and as such is the major vehicle for trade union involvement in the schools-industry field.


## THE ENVIRONMENT OF CHANGE

The schools-industry movement does not operate in a social, economic and political vacuum. Effectively there are two environments, one at the national level, the other at the local authority level. All the leading projects, the government agencies, the TUC and CBI, and the major firms are influenced by the 'national environment'. Discussions at this level concern themselves with both economic and educational questions. Thus Britain's GNP and the balance of payments problem join with youth unemployment and national systems of examining and profiling as areas of study and concern. The national environment is considerably influenced by the attitude of central government and some of the larger firms, simply because they provide the major financial backing for the schools-industry movement. Two examples illustrate the pattern of influence. In the late 1970s the schools-industry movement was dominated by central government's view that Britain's survival as a nation depended on the success of her traditional manufacturing sector. Industry meant manufacturing industry. During this period projects which did not share this view, and companies and organizations operating outside of this sector, took a low profile. As the government view has mellowed, the banks, building societies, and the whole of the service sector of the economy have risen to take on a key role in the movement. In a slightly similar fashion we can chart the growth in the importance of the small business sector. The rise in the esteem of this sector has led the schools-industry movement to embrace 'enterprise' as a key theme in its work. It has been estimated that almost one-fifth of all secondary schools now run business enterprises for some of their pupils (Jamieson, 1984).

The local environment for schools-industry work is naturally much more varied. The worries of Whitehall, or the CBI or even the TUC, do not necessarily intrude on life in schools. The startling fact that Britain is now running a deficit on its balance of trade in manufactured goods for the first time in its history, for example, does not impinge on the organization and curriculum of schools, save in those exceptional cases where the head teacher interprets this fact as having implications for the school.

What matters much more than national politics and economics is the local environment of the school. As we have argued, the local economic community can bring pressure to bear on schools through its influence on local councils and governing bodies, and through its control of employment opportunities. Surveying variations in schools-industry work in the nation's schools, it is certainly possible to make a case which suggests that both its amount and type are influenced by the socio-economic characteristics of the local area.

The urban north, for example, displays the greatest amount of schools-industry activity. The traditional industrial communities (places like Barnsley and Wakefield) have a sense of community and of ownership of their schools. Industrial capital *and* labour are strong local forces in these areas, and this is reflected in both business and the trade unions being prominent in the work. The suburban ring round the big cities, for example the outer London boroughs, also see schools-industry work flourishing. The sense of community is not as strong, but there is a lot of industrial and commercial activity in these areas on which the schools can draw. The amount of trade union involvement tends to reflect the political character of the area. In the inner city most people report that schools-industry work has an uphill task. There is precious little industry and commerce in much of the inner city, and the decay and disorganization of many of these areas present schools with many problems which are judged to be more important than drawing schools closer toward the industrial community. Although schools-industry work is bipartisan in political terms, it is true that Labour councillors do tend to be less committed—quite rightly they see the trade unions as poor relations to business in the majority of schools-industry activities. The Shire counties occupy a midpoint between the inner cities and the urban north in the schools-industry world. Town schools naturally find a greater range of opportunities than their more isolated rural counterparts. Although rural schools are surrounded by what is claimed to be Britain's most efficient industry, agriculture, it is interesting that schools-industry work has almost completely neglected this sector.

## UNEMPLOYMENT

No description of the environment of schools would be complete without a recognition of the importance of the employment environment. The relationship between high levels of youth unemployment and the schools-industry movement is a complex one. Many commentators are surprised that the movement has not withered away with the collapse of large sections of

Britain's manufacturing industry, and with it the job market for school-leavers. The impact of youth unemployment is marked by substantial local variations, and the position is masked by the variety and scope of the schemes designed to train or retrain prospective young workers. The effect of this, plus the widely reported reaction of teachers and students that 'unemployment is something that happens to somebody else', is to dilute the potential effect of unemployment on the schools. Many schools, even in areas of substantial youth unemployment, still cling to the traditional school-to-work scenario, and are happy to use the schools-industry organizations and projects to help their students become more competitive in job seeking.

We must also realize that the schools-industry movement as we have described it is a diverse movement. Not every group or organization working within its framework has been concerned with preparing young people for work. For example, those organizations who see their task in terms of explaining certain industrial and economic 'facts of life' to young people have been spurred on by unemployment. Such topics clearly need a lot of 'explaining' to young people. Furthermore, the organizations have, in general, adapted to the changing educational and economic scenario. Many of those who found themselves unhappily aboard the 'transition from school to working life' ship, have jumped ships and are now happily aboard the 'transition from school to adult life' boat, having made the happy 'discovery' that the qualities necessary for a well-adjusted adult life are more or less the same as those required in working life. A remarkable piece of seamanship by any standards.

## ENVIRONMENT MANAGEMENT—THE ROLE OF
## THE SCHOOLS-INDUSTRY LIAISON OFFICER

We have argued that in order to understand the schools-industry movement it is necessary to understand the heterogeneous nature of the various organizations which make up its 'membership', and the environments in which it operates. Our model is one of a variety of salesmen and persuaders trying to influence the schools. The schools 'buy' both what they feel they cannot avoid, and those 'goods' which they feel will be attractive and useful for their pupils.

One of the most significant developments in this model, and hence in the schools-industry movement, has been the rise of an intermediary between the schools and the environment. The schools-industry liaison officer (SILO), nearly always an employee of the Local Education Authority, acts as a broker, adviser and facilitator, both to the schools and the schools-industry organizations. The rise of the SILO has been dramatic. The first recorded post was in 1966 (Wood, 1983); by 1985 three-quarters of all LEAs had one. Their rise was fostered by the two big national projects, SCIP and UBI (over three-quarters of all the SILOs belong to the SCIP organization); by advice from the DES which recommended, 'that wherever practicable, one member of the CEO's staff should be given full-time responsibility for the promotion of schools-industry links' (DES, 1983); and finally, and most significantly, by funding from the Industry/Education Unit of the Department of Trade and Industry.

The schools-industry liaison officers are nearly all ex- or seconded teachers. This gives a strong clue to their major brief, which is to foster curriculum change in schools (or at least facilitate such change), so that the curriculum is more relevant to the needs of the pupils *and* the economy. Such a statement is fraught with difficulties and open to a large number of different interpretations. Different SILOs interpret their brief in very different ways. They are influenced by the policies of the LEA; the type and amount of local industry; the strength of the local trade union movement; the desires and interests of the local schools; and, not least, their affiliations to the various schools-industry organizations, particularly SCIP. Perhaps the most significant feature of the SILOs is that they are gradually dispensing with the services of the various national projects and running activities themselves. This is especially notable in the areas of work experience and the so-called mini-enterprises.

## CORPORATE HEGEMONY?

One of the great fears that teachers have about schools drawing closer to the industrial world is that the curriculum, and maybe even the ethos and organization of schools, will come to be dominated by business interests. Most teachers are surprised to learn that there are those who believe that business, or more properly the system of private enterprise, already dominates the education system (Bowles and Gintis, 1976).

Whether one believes these fears to be justified or not depends a great deal on the perspective adopted. At the level of the system it is possible to make a case, although rather a weak one in our view, to suggest that employers find the organization, curriculum and assessment system of schooling useful for their purposes. This is not of course to say either that education consciously organizes it in this way, or that employers are satisfied with the 'goodness of fit' between the two systems.

It is also possible to assemble some evidence to suggest that in the last few years many schools have moved closer to satisfying the needs of employers. Much of the evidence for this statement has been contained in the previous part of this essay. It could be argued that the pressure exerted by the schools-industry movement, particularly perhaps the adoption by so many LEAs of schools-industry liaison officers, is evidence enough of the system's desires to appease industrial criticism. In addition we might also note the rapid growth of prevocational and vocational courses in the schools, many of which require activities like work experience, and strongly recommend co-operation with local employers. Interestingly, many of these new courses are run and assessed not by the traditional university-dominated examining boards, but by bodies like the RSA, the City and Guilds, and the Business and Technician Education Council (B/TEC), which pride themselves on the fact that they are dominated by industrial and business interests. There have also been developments in pupil assessment which could be interpreted as in the interests of the business community. It is argued, for example, that criterion referencing rather than norm referencing will be much more helpful for industrial selectors. Pupil profiling, when it becomes a national system, might well help employers to make ever finer selections amongst prospective employees.

Despite this evidence, the view that the schools-industry movement represents some form of corporate hegemony is unconvincing, not least because it has not managed to make substantial changes in most secondary schools. The reason for this is that schools are relatively autonomous institutions, well used to resisting pressure from a wide variety of outside groupings. 'Academic freedom' and 'professional autonomy' have until now proved to be reasonably effective slogans with which to combat the demands of 'industrial relevance'.

A detailed observation of what happens 'on the ground' in schools-industry affairs is instructive. In the first place the employers are often divided among themselves: at the tactical level the needs and interests of different industrial sectors are not the same; big business is interested in a different range of problems from small business; banking has different interests from manufacturing industry, etc. We must also not forget the role of trade unions; although they are often poor relations, in practice they do offer some sort of check on the dominance of capital.

When the industrial world meets the schools it is argued that it often has divisions within its own ranks. We must also remember that the debate nearly always takes place on education's territory. The agenda is, 'How should the schools change?' Education displays all the normal advantages of 'home teams' by having a vastly superior knowledge of its own territory.

The result of all these 'disadvantages' is that very often employers become 'incorporated' into the educational world. We have described elsewhere the characteristic stages of schools-industry work (Jamieson and Lightfoot, 1982), whereby the suspicions and criticisms of employers are gradually transformed into qualified support for the system. This happens at all levels of schools-industry work: an interesting example is how the education/industry officers of some of the major companies, themselves usually ex-teachers, gradually become incorporated into the stage army of education. Many of them end up as apologists for the schools to their industrial and commercial colleagues.

## PEDAGOGIC LIBERATION?

It is one thing to cast doubt on the corporate hegemony thesis in schools-industry work, but quite another to claim that it is a potential source of pedagogic liberation. And yet this thesis looks at least as convincing as its corporate counterpart. The radical case rests on the following arguments. First, that the schools-industry movement underlines the important pedagogic fact that learning can and does take place outside of schools. After all, it was the deschooler Illich who proclaimed that: 'Access to reality constitutes a fundamental alternative in education to a system which only purports to teach *about* it' (Illich, 1973).

As part of its attempt to break down barriers between school and the outside world, the schools-industry advocates encourage schools to involve industrialists and trade unionists in the educational process. These 'adults other than teachers', as they are usually called, are rarely used in didactic teaching situations, at which they are often unskilled. Instead they are used in learning situations which make good use of their experience, and which place pupils in an active learning mode. Examples of this experiential learning include; role plays, games and simulations, as well as work experience.

One of the effects of the schools-industry movement then is to crack the edifice of didacticism in some schools. Another challenge is presented to an even more secure construction—the organization of learning within traditional academic subjects. Here radical teachers join with industrialists in claiming that 'real world' problems do not fall neatly into academic subject divisions. Some unlikely schools-industry activities have been heralded by radical teachers as 'breakthroughs'. While school-business enterprises can be used by Young Enterprise to give 'young people from all walks of life an idea of how business is organised and run in the Free World' (Bray, 1983), they can equally be used to give young people an opportunity to co-operate with each other, and to work things out for themselves without being constantly dominated by teachers (Jamieson, 1984).

Finally, we should note that even in the area of assessment, radical teachers can embrace many of the changes which are supported by industry. Pupil profiling is a good example. The industrialists believe that with more information about the young person, especially her skills and attitudes, the selection process will be eased. Many teachers welcome profiles because they see a chance of breaking out of the present system of 'graduated failure'. In a profile, pupils will be able to record their *achievements*, both in and out of school.


## CONCLUSION

We have argued that, despite the pressure exerted by the schools-industry movement on the schools, there has not been a radical move toward the 'industrial curriculum' in most secondary schools. We have explained this in terms of the power of the system to resist change, and its 'incorporation' of many industrial interests.

Before the advent of the TVEI initiative (the manner of whose introduction indicates that the government has learned a lot about changing the system) the schools-industry movement bore all the marks of what we might describe as the English model of curriculum change. Change depended on the ability of government and exemplars produced by various projects to convince educational professionals that change was necessary. Certainly there was more pressure, more projects, and certainly more money in this curriculum initiative than in most others. There was also evidence that, *compared with other curriculum movements*, the schools-industry initiative was pretty successful. It must be stressed that such success was not purely a function of a good sales campaign, but was also because many schools did genuinely want to make their curriculum more vocationally oriented, closer to the industrial world, more experience based—in short, what many of the schools and the schools-industry practitioners would describe as more 'relevant' to the modern world. In the schools-industry case demand has been at least as important as supply.

The success of the schools-industry movement has clearly not been sufficient for the government. The Technical and Vocational Education Initiative represents an altogether different approach to changing the curriculum. And however it is sold to the LEAs and the schools (there has been no shortage of takers), it looks to many like the first step on the road to government control of the curriculum. If this does turn out to be the case, it will not surprise many people that the dam was breached by a programme which wished to draw the schools nearer to the world of industry.

## REFERENCES

Atkinson, P., Rees, T.L., Shone, D. and Williamson, H. (1982) Social and life skills: the case of compensatory education, in Rees, T.L. and Atkinson, P. (eds.) *Youth Unemployment and State Intervention*, Routledge & Kegan Paul, London.
Bacon, R. and Eltis, W. (1976) *Britain's Economic Problem: Too Few Producers*, Macmillan, London.
Bowles, S. and Gintis, H. (1976) *Schooling in Capitalist America*, Routledge & Kegan Paul, London.
Bray, E. (1983) Mini-Co's in schools, in Watts, A.G. (ed.), *Work Experience in Schools*, Heinemann, London.
Cox, C.B. and Dyson, A.E. (eds.) (1969) *A Black Paper*, The Critical Quarterly Society, London.
Department of Education and Science (1983) Schools/industry liaison, letter to Chief Education Officers, SS/5/19/0127D, DES, London.
Floud, J. (1961) Social class factors in educational achievement, in Halsey, A.H. (ed.) *Ability and Educational Opportunity*, OECD, Paris.
HM Inspectors of Schools (1981) *Schools and Working Life*, DES, London.
HM Inspectors of Schools (1982) *Teacher Training and Preparation for Working Life*, DES, London.

Illich, I. (1973) The deschooled society in Buckman, P. (ed.) *Education without Schools,* Souvenir Press, London.
Jamieson, I.M. (1984) Schools and enterprise, in Watts, A.G. and Moran, P. (eds.) *Education for Enterprise,* CRAC, Cambridge.
Jamieson, I.M. and Lightfoot, M. (1982) *Schools and Industry,* Methuen, London.
Joseph, Sir Keith, Written parliamentary answer, 29 July 1982, contained in DES Circular letter SS 5/19/0127D 15 March 1983.
Moon, J. and Richardson, J.J. (1984) Policy making with a difference? the Technical and Vocational Education Initiative, in *Public Administration,* **26,** Spring.
Peters, T.J. and Waterman, R.H. Jnr. (1982) *In Search of Excellence: Lessons from America's Best Run Companies,* Harper & Row, New York.
Weiner, M. (1981) *English Culture and the Decline of Industrial Spirit,* Cambridge University Press, Cambridge.
Wood, B. (1983) *Schools Industry Liaison: The Development of Policy and the Role of the Schools Industry Officer,* Unpublished M.Ed. Thesis, Worcester College of Higher Education.

# 3

# The Background and Inception of the Technical and Vocational Education Initiative[1]

## ROGER DALE

The Technical and Vocational Education Initiative (originally known as the N (New) TVEI) was announced by the Prime Minister, Margaret Thatcher, in the House of Commons on 12 November 1982. She announced that 'in response to growing concern about existing arrangements for technical and vocational education for young people expressed over many years, not least by the National Economic Development Council', she had asked 'the chairman of the Manpower Services Commission together with the Secretaries of State for Education and Science, for Employment, and for Wales, to develop a pilot scheme to start by September 1983, for new institutional arrangements for technical and vocational education for 14–18-year-olds, within existing financial resources, and, where possible, in association with local authorities.'

That announcement came like a bolt from the blue to all the most directly interested parties. Neither the DES, the local education authority associations, the teacher professional organizations, nor even the MSC had been consulted before the announcement was made. It created an enormous furore not only by the manner of its delivery but also by what it appeared to threaten. The reference to 'new institutional arrangements', and to collaboration with local authorities 'where possible', gave rise to considerable fears that a new kind of institution was intended—or rather that something like the old

Specially commissioned for this volume. © The Open University, 1985.

[1] This article is intended as a broad survey of the TVEI programme, and contains little detail about the actual working of the initiative. Such details may be found in Dale (forthcoming).

technical school was to be revived. There were some grounds for these fears. David Young (then chairman of the MSC, now a Cabinet Minister, and together with Sir Keith Joseph and Norman Tebbit credited with producing the original plan) made it clear that MSC were in the last resort (if local education authorities did not co-operate in the scheme) prepared to set up their own schools, which he thought might even be called 'Young' schools (*Education*, 19, 26 November 1982).

However, local authority resistance crumbled very rapidly (though complaints about lack of consultation continued) and their collaboration in the scheme was assured with Mr Young's announcement that the membership of the National Steering Group to be set up to run the initiative 'would reflect the key part the education service would play in the pilot projects' (*Education*, 26 November 1982).

The TVEI scheme emerged as

> a pilot scheme; within the education system; for young people of both sexes; across the ability range; voluntary. Each project must provide a full-time programme; offer a progressive four-year course combining general with technical and vocational education; commence at 14 years; be broadly based; include planned work experience; lead to nationally recognised qualifications. Each project and the initiative as a whole must be carefully monitored and evaluated. The purpose of the scheme is to explore and test ways of organizing and managing readily replicable programmes of technical and vocational education for young people across the ability range (MSC, 1984).

In his letter to all education authorities in England and Wales, inviting them to submit applications, David Young amplified this framework by indicating that the general objective was to 'widen and enrich the curriculum in a way that will help young people prepare for the world of work, and to develop skills and interests, including creative abilities, that will help them to lead a fuller life and to be able to contribute more to the life of the community'. Secondly, he suggested that 'we are in the business of helping students to "learn to learn". In a time of rapid technological change, the extent to which particular occupational skills are required will change. What is important about this initiative is that youngsters should receive an education which will enable them to adapt to the changing occupational environment.'

Sixty-six LEAs applied to be included in the project and fourteen were chosen (the originally planned number was enlarged to ensure better geographical coverage). A central feature of the scheme is that these authorities then signed contracts with MSC for the delivery of the project outlined in their application. These projects were all drawn up to match the guidelines contained in David Young's letter, but they differed considerably from each other in philosophy, numbers of schools involved (though most schemes included between five and eight schools and colleges of further education) and the number of pupils to be involved (though the funding basis assumed five annual cohorts of 250 pupils per authority). Some of these differences and their implications are elaborated more fully below. Each local project is responsible to a local steering group made up of representatives of both sides of industry, educational interests, voluntary organizations and so on. The steering groups report to the TVEI Unit in the MSC and to the local authority.

Twice as many Conservative as Labour authorities applied; Labour authorities refused to submit bids on the grounds that the scheme would both be divisive by reintroducing some form of selection into comprehensive education, and have a narrowing, excessively vocationalizing effect on the curriculum. These have been the dominant criticisms of the TVEI scheme throughout its short history. At first, the pilot nature of the scheme received a great deal of emphasis. Critics in the House of Commons (where questions on TVEI were answered both by Employment and Education ministers) and elsewhere were typically told not to become too anxious or worried about what was after all only a small pilot scheme. And yet, scarcely three months after the announcement of the first group of pilot LEAs and before the projects had started, it was announced that the scheme would be extended, with another £20 million, in addition to the original £7 million available to bring in another forty or so (in the end forty-four more authorities were accepted) LEAs in September 1984. And then, in October 1984, a further extension of the scheme was announced to start in September 1985. The indications are that all those who apply in this round will be successful, leaving only a residue of Labour authorities opting out, on broadly the same grounds as they originally gave.

This is an exceedingly brief account of a very complex process, which is still evolving. In the remaining sections of the paper I want to go on to discuss the background and origins of TVEI, to examine the processes through which it was implemented, and to address the question of 'What is TVEI?' Before I do that, though, it is important to point out some key features of TVEI as an education innovation.

TVEI does not follow any of the three main routes of bringing about major educational change in Britain, either in the nature of its aims or in its methods. It is neither a programme drawn up by and in consultation with practising educators, aimed at improving the content and/or delivery of (parts of) the school curriculum (the Schools Council model); nor does it follow the Plowden, Advisory Committee, model, where representatives of a wide range of appropriate interests join with the 'great and the good' to scrutinize, and recommend a series of more or less major changes; nor does it follow the model of legislative change, which encouraged comprehensive schooling, for instance, or raised the school-leaving age. Rather, it might be argued, it follows a business or commercial model, moving resources into a new 'line' when the existing one is proving ineffective. At the centre of its aims is improving the service to a particular group of customers, clients and consumers—it does not seek to improve the service to those already seen as (too) well catered for. Its mode of operation is executive rather than legislative or advisory. And it is singularly unencumbered either by the professional experts, or by the great and the good—there are no latter-day Lords Vaizey or (Michael) Young in TVEI.

TVEI is then a political intervention, in the sense that it was introduced into the education system from outside, albeit with the acquiescence or even encouragement of the Secretary of State for Education (though without even the knowledge of his department officials, or any other part of the educational apparatus, national or local). Though in the end the co-operation of the majority of LEAs was secured—at least to the extent of making themselves contractually accountable for disposing of very large sums of money for specified purposes (though, as I shall show below, it cannot be assumed that these purposes were necessarily inimical to them)—it is clear from David Young's comments quoted above that the scheme would have been introduced anyway (though whether it could have succeeded without the co-operation of the education service is a matter of fascinating, if now futile, debate).

Another crucial feature of TVEI is its size and scope. It now involves the majority of education authorities (though, not, of course, the majority of schools or pupils) in the country and provides unprecedentedly large amounts of money for those involved. Its objective is not merely the improvement or updating of a particular aspect of the school curriculum—although this is undoubtedly part of its intention—but the redirection and restructuring of the school experiences of a large proportion of pupils. This redirecting and restructuring is aimed at bringing schools into a closer relationship with the world outside them, especially, though not exclusively, 'the world of work'. This will involve making 'the vocational' rather than 'the academic' the central purpose and criterion of what a considerable proportion—if not all—children learn in school. In both these aspects, then, its extra-educational, political origins, and its funding and ambitions, TVEI is quite unlike any curriculum innovation we have seen in this country before.

TVEI also differs from what has gone before in the pattern, process and pace of curricular change it involves. It represents an obvious and deliberate break with the essentially incremental, apparently haphazard, pattern which had typified educational change. It represents as much a break with as continuity with existing provision, seeking to renew or even replace it as much as building on it. Its size and its ambitions also push it towards being comprehensive rather than piecemeal.

The accepted pattern is challenged, too, through its operation at the margins of the school, both financially and educationally. That is to say, TVEI gains maximum 'bang for a buck' from all its funding being devoted to additional items, and none of it to the continuing basic cost of running the school, which accounts for nearly all the funding it receives, leaving very little available for 'development'. Educationally, its funding and the conditions attaching to it mean that, at least formally, the school has to adjust to the innovation rather than the other way round.

The process of change is not wholly dependent on persuasion and the marshalling of voluntary effort in the schools involved. LEAs and schools are contractually accountable for implementing the changes they propose to introduce. They must be able to demonstrate that the material and human resources they have bought with TVEI money are being used, at least preferentially, with the pupils, and for the purposes, specified in the contract. A second major difference is that formal authority for the direction of the project is vested not in the schools, or the LEA or the MSC, alone, but in the local steering group (on which, of course, all three parties are represented, along with both sides of industry). A third difference is that the projects are also monitored by members of an advisory team within the TVEI Unit. All those appointed so far have had extensive experience within the education service, and they appear to see their role as much as a supportive and advisory as an evaluative one.

Finally, it is clear from the timetable outlined above that the TVEI has been introduced at quite unprecedented speed. Scarcely nine months after the first, entirely unheralded, announcement, the scheme was operating in fourteen LEAs, who had had two months to prepare their applications and who learned that they had been successful barely a term before the programmes had to start. The pace has hardly relaxed since then, certainly in the schools, as the implications of those very rapid decisions became transformed into timetable, resource, administrative and pedagogic problems all requiring almost immediate responses.

## THE BACKGROUND TO TVEI

Its unique, secret and personal origins make it difficult to point with any conviction of accuracy to the sources and diagnosis that lay behind the TVEI proposal. Nevertheless, it is possible to infer a good deal about that diagnosis. It has two main elements. One is that what is taught in schools has to be changed. The other is that the process of changing what is taught in schools has itself to be changed. Both these elements were, of course, central to the 'Great Debate' on education of 1977, and they remained important, though not exclusive, components of the diagnosis which five years later produced the TVEI.

The influence of the teaching profession over what went on in education had already begun to decline before the institution of the Great Debate, under the influence of falling school rolls (and consequent loss of union 'muscle'), the ideological onslaught on the alleged consequences of a teacher-dominated system, encapsulated in the Black Papers, and a general feeling of dissatisfaction that education had failed to deliver what it had promised, socially, politically and economically, and for which it had claimed ever-growing funds. In particular, the education system had at the very least done little to forestall or inhibit the county's economic decline. And this apparent failure of the education system was laid very much at the door of the teachers, especially following the William Tyndale affair, which led to teachers being identified as the major culprits in this situation. This was possible in large part because of the 'licensed autonomy' which gave them great influence over the kinds of changes that should take place in the education system (see Dale, 1979, 1981).

A clear recognition of the perceived need to curtail 'teacher power' was inscribed in the very format of the Great Debate. As Bates puts it:

> the Great Debate reflected a trend towards defining and limiting the boundaries of teacher autonomy. The very initiation of a public debate on education, involving the unprecedented consultation of industrial organizations and parents as well as educational organizations, served as an explicit reminder to the teaching profession that the curriculum was not solely their responsibility to determine.... Thus the Great Debate, irrespective of its content, simply as a means of intervening in education helped to change the political context in which educational issues were discussed (Bates, 1984, p. 199).

That teachers' licensed autonomy affected not only the process of educational change, but also its content was, of course, a central theme of the Great Debate. A clear tension was discerned there between teachers' professional interest and the interests of the wider society, and especially of industry. This professional interest led to an over-emphasis on the academic and a matching neglect of the vocational aspect of schooling.

The argument that it is essential to change this emphasis, and the stress on the 'need' to bring education and industry closer together, to attach the former more closely to the needs of the latter has, of course, been the object of a 'recurrent debate' (Reeder, 1979) in English education over the course of this century. This is not the place to go through that debate [which is developed briefly in the Introduction to this book, and more fully in Reeder (1979) and Esland and Cathcart (1981)], while useful accounts of American experience which suggest that education is called in to solve a range of social and economic problems, are given in Grubb and Lazerson (1981) and McGowan and Cohen (1971).

Beck has convincingly argued that through the second half of the seventies industry's contribution to this recurrent debate took a dual form. On the one hand, larger employers and, significantly, the Department of Industry were putting forward the criticism that, the education system's longstanding academic bias 'had played a major part in creating and maintaining the situation in which wealth creation, the profit motive and engineering were accorded less status in Britain than in most other manufacturing countries' (Beck, 1983, p. 221). On the other hand, a campaign against alleged declining standards and discipline, generated mainly in the press, pointed to the negative consequences for pupils' attitudes to work and authority of progressive teaching methods, teacher autonomy and certain aspects of comprehensive reorganization.

However, it was quite clear that it was not enough merely to advise, counsel and tinker. Stripped of its academic bias, the education system would not automatically revert to some pristine 'economy-friendly' state; a positive alternative was required. This alternative, heavily implicit in the Great Debate, and explicit before and after it, remains vocational education.

The problem is that vocational education is a very slippery and ambiguous concept. This is because it is defined in opposition, or contrast, to what it is hoped it will supplant. Thus vocational education is called on in the Great Debate and Green Paper to save a system with an inappropriate curriculum bias, low standards, and insufficient and ineffective links with industry. Hence, vocational education comes to be associated with three quite distinct purposes, making pupils more able to get jobs, making them better performers in jobs, and making them more aware of the world of work, and the workings of the economy which awaits them.

The term 'vocational education', then, covers three different and separate —though not necessarily mutually incompatible—aspects of the diagnosis produced by the Great Debate. It is to counter (a) the teacher-based progressive ideology which allegedly leads to a neglect of, or even contempt for, rigour and standards, and produces pupils with attitudes inimical to the disciplinary and moral requirements of many employers, who prefer therefore to offer jobs to older, more mature and more 'stable', if less qualified, people; (b) the fact that the things that pupils are taught at school are inappropriate, and often do not equip them to do the jobs they are offered; (c) the fact that they do not know enough about the world of work, and especially about the economic importance of industry. This applies almost as much to those who will enter other economic sectors as to those who will remain unemployed (see Moore, 1984). As an answer to all these shortcomings a more vocationally-oriented education consequently becomes even more difficult to define and to prescribe in detail.

The diagnosis contained within or implied by the Great Debate does not, however, exhaust the diagnosis which underlies TVEI. There are at least two factors which led to the need for its supplementation. First of all, though the diagnosis was at least superficially clear, very little had happened between 1977 and 1982 to shift schools in the required direction; many of the criticisms contained in the Great Debate and Green Paper still held good. And second, over that period there had been a quite dramatic increase in youth unemployment, as well as continuing expansion of 'high-tech' industry. Both these factors were incorporated into the diagnosis which we can infer underlay TVEI.

Other articles in this volume focus directly on the MSC's responses to the growth in youth unemployment, and I do not intend to discuss them at any great length here. It is clear, though, that the work that the MSC had done in response to youth unemployment influenced the thinking behind TVEI. (This is not to say that because TVEI is located in the MSC it automatically parallels MSC's policies for young people post-school in school. It is clear that

TVEI is not 'YTS in the schools'—though many critics originally assumed that it would be.) Essentially, the recognition that youth unemployment was too important and, certainly in the wake of the Toxteth riots, too potentially dangerous to be left to the market, produced a dual response. On the one hand, it greatly intensified moves towards providing far more training. This was an original purpose of the MSC, which became less prominent during the period of the Youth Opportunities Programme, but resurfaced again very powerfully in the New Training Initiative and the Youth Training Scheme. This latter scheme was held by many (see the article by Farley in this volume) to contain the seeds of the comprehensive training programme which it was held Britain, in contrast to its competitors, and especially West Germany, had never had. The possibility that this kind of training could be built into a single, coherent 14–18 scheme, certainly seems to underly some TVEI projects.

The other part of the MSC response to youth unemployment is 'vocational preparation'. This consists of programmes aimed at attuning young people to the world of work, though they may never experience it directly themselves. It is a series of solutions to what Offe calls 'the problem of institutional "storage" of the portion of the social volume of labour power which (because of conjunctural and structural changes) cannot be absorbed by the demands generated by the labour market' (1984, p. 99). The problem is essentially one of keeping the unemployed employable, of keeping them available for employment when employment is not available for them. It is tackled in two main ways. One is through programmes of ersatz work experience (see Watts, 1983). In projects of vocational preparation this work experience is a vehicle not so much for learning skills or applying knowledge learned in school, but for learning something of what it feels like to be employed. The other main response is the development of programmes of 'social and life skills'. One aspect of these programmes stresses the importance of acquiring non-academic, interpersonal skills which are useful in getting and keeping jobs, especially white collar jobs; content focuses on how to behave at interviews, how to take and give messages and instructions, and so on. The other aspect stresses adjustment to a likely long period of unemployment, coping with its impact on personal, social and family relationships.

The other major strand of influence of the MSC's experience in youth training and youth unemployment is rather more difficult to pin down. It is essentially a new kind of pedagogy, rooted in the work of the Further Education Unit, whose publications have done much to define this approach. There is space here to do little more than list some of these shifts (they are elaborated more fully in Dale (forthcoming)), but it is worthwhile to do so because they are evidently beginning to affect the work of TVEI schools, especially through the introduction into schools of courses leading to qualifications of the Business and Technician Education Council, the City and Guilds of London Institute, the Royal Society of Arts, and other bodies whose work had previously been confined to the post-compulsory sector. This 'new FEU pedagogy' involves, then, among other things, a move towards teaching courses rather than subjects, 'experiential' and 'problem solving' rather than 'academic' learning, criterion rather than norm referenced assessment, competence rather than age-related courses, the introduction of profiling on a wide scale and qualifications that are 'work-related'. These features are not, of course, being taken on wholesale by schools (though it is important to note the desire of B/TEC and CGLI to gain very much more than a foothold in the pre-16 curriculum; see 'Schools to be offered new practical curriculum' *TES* 6 January 1984), but it is clear that some of them, especially perhaps profiling (which is a part of all TVEI projects), are being introduced across a range of schools.

One final aspect of the experience of the MSC's youth programmes, which crosscuts all those discussed so far should be mentioned at this point. This is the connection between practicality and relevance, and student motivation. Those 'turned off' schools by an academic diet are frequently reported as blooming when carrying out relevant or practical work, and to become 'different people' on work experience.

The third major strand of the diagnosis which appears to underly TVEI is the educational consequences of the pace and nature of technological change. Again, the issues are well known, and by no means exclusive to TVEI, and I will do no more than mention them here. The educational implications of the pace of technological change have usually been derived from an assumption that it will mean that very few people are likely to stay in the same job, or even the same broad area of work, all their lives. There is a consequent need for 'education for flexibility', and specifically an emphasis on 'generic' rather than 'specific' skills. This does not seem to have been nearly such a prominent feature in TVEI, however, as those associated with the *content* of technological change, and especially the growth of Information Technology. There are at least three assumed consequences of this growth that are built into the diagnosis. First, it is held that future employment prospects are likely to be most propitious in IT based industry and commerce. Second, even those who are not employed in IT related jobs will live their lives in a society where relationships of all kinds, and especially of individuals to institutions, will be transformed by IT. And third, teaching and learning themselves will make ever-increasing use of IT, altering both what it is possible to teach, and how it is possible to teach it. These three features combine to place a heavy emphasis on IT in TVEI.

The three aspects of the diagnosis which I have identified so far, the legacy of the Great Debate, the rise of youth unemployment, and the consequences of technological change, are by no means exclusive to TVEI. They are, rather, part of the *zeitgeist* and I have merely tried to indicate the particular emphases which seem to underly the specific TVEI diagnosis. However, there is one further element, which underlies much of the distinctiveness of the TVEI diagnosis and it is peculiar to TVEI. This derives from David Young's close personal association with the Jewish charity ORT, the Organization for Rehabilitation through Training, which, it is clear, provided something of a model for TVEI. 'ORT's philosophy is to incorporate job specific training into a broad education beginning at the age of 14, with an emphasis on the individual pupil. . . . The British ORT trust (of which David Young was an original trustee) was founded in 1980 out of a concern that schools here were failing to develop the potential of a large proportion of their pupils, and a desire to make education more relevant to the world outside, by developing practical and marketable skills' (Hofkins 1984, p. 180).

## PUTTING TVEI INTO PRACTICE

While most of the elements of the diagnosis which produced TVEI were common currency, they had had rather little impact on the education system. Privately sponsored programmes like Project Trident, which concentrated on providing work experience for school pupils, and Young Enterprise, which aimed to show them how business worked, had had some impact, (see the article by Jamieson in this volume), but neither they nor any more official efforts seemed likely to bring about the kind of redirection of the education system called for in the Great Debate and Green Paper.

There are a number of reasons for this. Among the more important are:

1. The DES's constitutional position prevented it from making central interventions in the school curriculum. It had therefore to rely on what it could achieve by means of advice, persuasion and whatever pressure it could bring to bear.
2. The funding base of schools made them less vulnerable to the kind of incursions that the MSC had been able to make into the curriculum and structure of colleges of further education.
3. It is by no means certain that the DES's own field representatives and organic intellectuals, the HMI, were convinced either of the correctness of the diagnosis or of the value and appropriateness for schools of the approaches contained within MSC youth programmes.
4. The schools and teachers had always quite explicitly opposed attempts to divert them in a more employment-related direction. They, too, did not accept the diagnosis, which they felt made them scapegoats for the nation's economic decline.

Thus, while the problem of the kind of education required by the diagnosis outlined above was being taken seriously, and a range of possible solutions was available, the problem of school, teacher and education system autonomy and accountability remained. There was not in the existing framework a way of reorienting schools in the desired direction. That is why the MSC had to be given the job of delivering the TVEI.

The fact of the MSC rather than DES control of the programme does also have effects on its delivery and implementation similar to its influence on the content outlined above. These effects are rooted in the different constitutions of the two bodies. The DES is a department of State headed by a cabinet minister politically accountable through Parliament to the *electorate*. It operates according to a structured, bureaucratic, rule-following model. The MSC, on the other hand, is a corporate body, made up of people representing particular *interests*, particularly the two sides of industry. This means that any decisions and actions it takes can be assumed already to have the approval of those they affect (insofar as they are represented on the commission); those actions and decisions do not have to go through further consultative, participative discussion stages—which, of course, means that MSC is able to act much more quickly than DES. MSC's operating model, similarly, differs from the DES's. Rather than being bureaucratic and process-oriented, it is technocratic or even commercial; for MSC, achieving results is the criterion of action, while the DES is bound by the need for accurate rule-following. This means that DES can only bring about major change by changing the rules; for MSC, it is much more straightforward. Furthermore, certainly in the education area, MSC has operated more like a fire-brigade than a police force. That is to say, it ranges freely across the terrain, without permanent attachment to any part of it, with the possibility of withdrawing altogether, and with no built-in continuing commitment to the area. Thus not only is it able to introduce different kinds of programmes, it is also able to do so less hampered by the ramifications they may have for the rest of the service.

What the education service was confronted with when TVEI was announced, then, was a broadly familiar package to be delivered by quite new means to a body operating with a style, expectations, and under a set of constraints, quite different from those it was used to. How the LEAs and schools reacted to this situation, and the effect of that reaction on the shape of TVEI in practice, will make up the remainder of this article.

For the essential point is, of course, that being acquainted with the origin and framework of the project does not necessarily tell us a great deal about how it works. It certainly does not tell us conclusively and comprehensively what TVEI is. This is so for the general reason that practically every study ever published of an educational or curriculum innovation concludes that the form it actually takes is different from what was intended, that the process of implementation itself alters the shape and emphasis of the project. It is also true in the particular case of TVEI for the reason both that, as suggested in the last section, the diagnosis is a fairly broad and flexible one, which does not entail or specify particular remedies for particular problems, and that there was no pressure from MSC for LEAs to conform to particular kinds of programme in their submissions. They had, of course, to fit in with the guidelines, but there was a clear acceptance, and even encouragement, of the diversity across the local projects; this is demonstrated clearly in the first fourteen projects selected, which differ very considerably from each other in their interpretation of the common guidelines, their institutional arrangements and so on. Even where the same subjects appear near universally, like Technology or Business Studies, the level and content at which they are to be approached differs across the schemes.

What TVEI is, then, in any particular LEA or school, is the outcome of continuing interplay between the requirements of participation in the initiative, as spelled out in the authority's contract with the MSC, and what existed before, and continues to exist alongside, TVEI in the authority and schools. TVEI has to be accommodated to the existing patterns of practice; however great the sums of money involved in any particular local project may appear as extra funding, they are a very small proportion of the overall budget, and certainly not sufficient to cause an LEA to completely reorganize itself as the condition of accepting TVEI money—though this is rather less true at the level of the school.

It will be useful to go very briefly through the structures and processes through which the design and implementation of local TVEI schemes have to pass to get an idea how, and how far, the broad guidelines of the initiative are shaped to meet local requirements, conditions and traditions. The obvious place to start is the LEA's decision to prepare an application for participation in TVEI. It seems that in each of the three rounds of TVEI there was in some authorities a great deal of discussion over whether to bid for TVEI or not. As I stated above, the main grounds of opposition (apart from the initial, and continuing, anger over the manner of announcing the scheme) were that the scheme was divisive and that it would have a narrowing effect on the curriculum. One further objection was that the money came from the MSC, which led to fears of a take-over of the school system similar to that which it was felt MSC was carrying out in the further education sector. The continuing strength of these objections is apparent in the fact that twenty-one LEAs in England and Wales and four in the north of Scotland are still refusing to submit bids for TVEI money. So why did the majority of LEAs apply to take part in the scheme? After all, the initially hostile reception to the scheme was practically universal. The answer is, undoubtedly, because of the money. Though some LEAs were already carrying out TVEI-like projects, and others were eager to do so, it is unlikely that so many of them would have volunteered to take part in a scheme with the aims of TVEI if there had not been such large sums of money involved. At a time of falling rolls and declining funding for education, most authorities felt that they could not afford not to bid for the TVEI money, and they invested much time and effort in preparing their bids in an extremely short time. The extent to which local authorities were *only* 'doing it for the money', i.e. the nature of their commitment to the principles of TVEI, varied considerably. There are some missionaries among the first round of TVEI authorities, and also perhaps some who were hoping to be able to 'take the money and run'.

Differences between the various schemes deriving from the nature of the authority's ideological commitment to it became wider through the process of the preparation of the bid. At least three rather different models, with different consequences for the eventual shape of the scheme, appear to have been followed. In some authorities, the initial approach from MSC was passed to the authority's senior officer dealing with further education, because he or she was the person responsible for all contact with MSC. This led in some of those cases to the scheme being drawn up within the further education section of the LEA and consequently inscribed with at least some of the elements of the FEU pedagogy mentioned above. A different pattern, and one which I suspect was much more common among the second round authorities who had a little longer than the first round to prepare their bid, was to devolve responsibility for drawing up the scheme to a consortium, or competing consortia, of heads in the authority. These groups were obviously likely to be primarily committed to getting what they could out of the scheme for the schools. A third pattern was for the authority to select the schools to take part in the scheme first, and draw up a proposal in collaboration with them. A further dimension of difference within this pattern comes from the different criteria used to select the schools. Some TVEI schools have been included because they have demonstrated that they could make it work, others because they are thought to need a new challenge. In some cases it has been used to equalize provision across the authority by bringing extra resources to the worst-off schools, in others it has been used to smooth school amalgamation. In yet others, TVEI funds have gone to the schools in the areas of the most powerful councillors.

So, just as the guidelines did not clearly imply or promote any particular kind of scheme, nor did they suggest any 'profiles for the TVEI school'. In this situation, though their initial motivation may have been the money, when it came to preparing the applications which showed how the money would be used, local authorities fitted the requirements of TVEI to their own particular circumstances. How they did this varied with the way the bid was prepared, but typically TVEI money provided solutions to other problems in addition to that of changing the provision of technical and vocational education according to a specified set of guidelines.

It should not be assumed, however, that LEAs have been able to take on TVEI without cost, that they are doing nothing they would not have done anyway, given the funding. At the simplest level, it seems highly unlikely that any LEA would have been willing to suggest, or able to get away with, such an uneven distribution of such large resources across its schools. The concentration of those very significant extra resources within, in most cases, a very small proportion of their schools, has undoubtedly created major problems for LEAs. It seems unlikely, too, that LEAs would voluntarily have surrendered even that part of their control of what goes on in their schools which is required by participation in TVEI.

TVEI's reception in the schools largely parallels that in the LEAs. Initial suspicion of its background and purpose mixed with morale levels depressed through the eighties by curtailment of funding and poor career prospects to leave schools uncertain about what was required, and also about what they might have to concede. In this situation TVEI represented for most schools almost the only prospect of funded curriculum development at all, let alone of such lavish funding, and like the LEAs, this made it difficult for those identified by whatever processes the LEA used as TVEI schools to say no to participation in the project. As with the LEAs it is difficult to point to a typical school reaction to TVEI. Some of those involved were clearly very anxious to be included in the scheme, others were wary of it; some staffs were divided on it, while others were agnostic. Schools' motives were as varied as LEAs, but again the money and resources involved were critical factors.

The TVEI schools have, though, had to change in a number of ways, and while certainly almost every one of them I have consulted insists they are doing nothing they would not anyway have wanted to do if the funding had been available, it is not so clear that the *particular* changes entailed by TVEI would have been at the top of their priority list, or that, given a free hand, they would have spent the available money in precisely, or even broadly, the same areas.

Though the changes within the schools following the inception of TVEI vary, they are brought about by a similar set of contractual requirements. These include the need to identify a 'cohort' of TVEI pupils who must be given priority access to the human and material resources purchased with TVEI money (there appears to be little restriction on their use beyond this cohort, provided that their priority is not infringed). This does not mean, incidentally, that the cohort has to be identifiable within the school. There are certainly some schools where the named TVEI pupils are not aware of their status, and where those who teach them are not aware of it either. This does, though, appear to be an aspect of the scheme which is closely monitored by the TVEI Unit in MSC, perhaps because it is one most open to exploitation by those who would 'take the money and run'. Another very closely monitored aspect of the scheme which has considerable implications for the schools involved is the requirement to move towards ending or at least minimizing the sex-stereotyping of subjects. TVEI authorities and schools have been subjected to a fair degree of pressure in this area. Protests of good intentions have not been sufficient; evidence of practical steps in the required direction has to be provided. The other relatively 'new' element brought into TVEI schools has been profiling, and here there have been great differences in the stance adopted by LEAs and schools, from those who looked for a suitable off-the-peg package, to those who have devoted enormous amounts of time and effort to preparing sophisticated and comprehensive systems.

At one level, indeed, the most immediate and obvious impact of TVEI on schools has been the vast amount of extra work it has involved for staff, especially, but not only, those directly involved in the project. They have been involved not just in 'new' or 'additional' projects, like attempting to mitigate sex-stereotyping, or creating a profiling system, but also in what they would, pre-TVEI, have recognized as hard core curriculum development, in drawing up new courses to fit in with the local interpretations of TVEI. And though this has in some schools reinforced any divisiveness inherent in TVEI, in rather more it has provided a boost to morale, and rekindled the professional fires of a large group of teachers, many of which had been dampened, apparently for good, by the depressed state of the profession in the years before TVEI came on the scene.

In the end, the surest guide to what comprises TVEI in any particular LEA or school is what that LEA or school was like before November 1982. But though LEAs and schools have not been forced to do anything they would not have wanted to do, given the funding, this does not mean that they are spending TVEI money as they would have, given a free hand. To this extent, at least, the initiative has succeeded in shifting the pattern of education in the schools involved in it.


## NOTE

This article is intended as a broad survey of the TVEI programme, and contains little detail about the actual working of the initiative. Such details may be found in Dale (forthcoming).


## REFERENCES

Bates, Inge (1984) From vocational guidance to life skills: Historical perspectives on careers education, in Bates, I. *et al.* (ed.), *Schooling for the Dole?* Macmillan, London, pp. 170–219.

Dale, Roger (1979) The politicization of school deviance: the case of William Tyndale, in Barton, L. and Meighan, R. (eds.), *Schools, Pupils and Deviance*, Nafferton, Driffield, pp. 95–112.

Dale, Roger (1981) Schools, accountability and William Tyndale, in Dale, R. *et al.* (eds.), *Education and the State: Vol. II Politics, Patriarchy and Practice*, Falmer Press, Sussex.

Dale, Roger (forthcoming) Examining the gift horse's teeth: an analysis of TVEI, in Barton, L. and Walker, S. (eds.), *Youth, Unemployment and Schooling*, Open University Press, Milton Keynes.

Esland, Geoff, and Cathcart, Heather (1981) *Education and the Corporate Economy: Course E353 Unit 2*, Open University Press, Milton Keynes.

Grubb, W. Norton and Lazerson, Marvin (1981) Vocational solutions to youth problems: the persistent frustrations of the American experience, *Educational Analysis*, 3, 2, 91–103.

Hofkins, Diane (1984) ORT: confidence through skills, *Education*, 163, 5, 100.

McGowan, Eleanor E. and Cohen, David K. (1977) 'Career Education'—reforming school through work, *Public Interest*, 46, Winter, pp. 28–47.

Manpower Services Commission (1984) *Technical and Vocational Education Initiative Operating Manual*.

Moore, Robert (1984) Schooling and the world of work, in Bates, I. *et al.* (ed.) *Schooling for the Dole?*, Macmillan, London, pp. 65–103.

Offe, Claus (1984) *Contradictions of the Welfare State*, Heinemann, London.

Reeder, David (1979) A recurring debate: Education and industry, in Berbaum, G. (ed.), *Schooling in Decline*, Macmillan, London, pp. 115–48.

Weiner, Martin (1981) *English Culture and The Decline of the Industrial Spirit*, Cambridge University Press, Cambridge.

# 4

# Privatization of Industry and the Nationalization of Youth

## DENIS GLEESON

### INTRODUCTION

Until recently the further education activities of 16–19-year-olds remained a neglected area of sociological enquiry, FE's voluntaristic and entrepreneurial character perhaps reflecting the low status image traditionally associated with technical education. With a few notable exceptions (Robinson, 1968; Venables, 1967; Tipton, 1973), research in the sociology of education has tended to focus on schooling with little or no attention paid to the activities of industrial trainers. However, the legacy of youth unemployment and the rise of the MSC has ensured that the debate about FE and training is unlikely to remain unchanged. Once considered an educational backwater, FE has today entered the forefront of educational debate. In the two decades following publication of the Crowther Report (1959) much has happened to the non-advanced FE sector, not least to the expansion and diversification of its links with industry, student intake and curricular arrangements. Since then, however, the degree of decentralized development has been increasingly brought under control by centralist measures designed to incorporate FE within the wider context of state-training policy (White Paper, 1984). Moreover, recent attempts to reshape LEA and college budgets to make them more responsive to MSC initiatives has ensured the central place of government in structuring national priorities in the sphere of further education and training.

During a period in which government has reduced support for publicly

Specially commissioned for this volume. © The Open University, 1985.
A modified version of this paper was first presented at the International Sociology of Education Conference, *Youth Unemployment and Schooling*, Westhill College, Birmingham, January 1985.

owned industry and pursued an aggressive policy on privatization, training policy remains a conspicuous exception. As spending on the 'New Training Initiative' (MSC, 1981) tops £4½b in 1986, a 'watershed' in training policy has been reached, whereby the state has now taken over the responsibility of training from employers (Ryan, 1984). At a time when the efficiency of state enterprise is viewed with considerable scepticism it is somewhat ironic that government policy should effectively nationalize training, thereby removing it from the private sector and placing it in the hands of the civil service. It should be recognized, however, that training policy does not simply represent a response to unemployment but is also designed to alter relations in the work place in favour of employers (Fairley and Grahl, 1983). From this viewpoint, training has a closer relationship with private enterprise than might first appear; it also represents an important political mechanism through which labour is made ready and available for work. This matter will be taken up later.

For present purposes what remains less than clear is the part FE is likely to play within the more centralized arrangements of training. At the moment FE is at the crossroads between its voluntaristic tradition and the newer compulsory elements that have come to challenge it. If in 1968 the non-advanced sector of FE could be described as 'uncharted territory' (Robinson, 1968), this sector has now taken on a more systematic appearance. Paradoxically, the rise of youth unemployment has not only initiated far reaching reforms, but it has also breathed fresh life into many of Crowther's original proposals, notably in relation to the extension of FE 'for all'. If, however, Crowther's ghost would appear to be alive and well, considerable ambiguity exists about how far FE and training represents an 'alternative route' or 'second chance' for those students traditionally denied access to its ranks, but now included through MSC provision. This paper considers two interrelated aspects of this problem. The first concerns changing patterns of student participation in FE and the structuring of youth opportunities in the labour market via various types of curricular experience, notably 'basic skills' and 'generic skills' training. The second concerns the ways in which political and economic policy find their expression in the curriculum and organization of FE, thereby shaping the wider social relations between FE, industry and the state. At the outset it is perhaps important to say something about recent developments in FE and training and its incorporation within more centralized forms of control.

## CONTINUITY AND CHANGE IN FE AND TRAINING

Despite the recent controversy surrounding the way in which the MSC 'bought its way' into FE (Moos, 1984), its entry has been achieved relatively easily. If, at one level, this can simply be explained in terms of cash input, at another many educationalists, trade unionists and others welcomed MSC intervention as a progressive means of extending training provision to school-leavers traditionally denied access to its ranks. Rising youth unemployment and the slow response of the DES in the mid-1970s prompted some commentators to view MSC overtures in a reformist light (Watts, 1983; Hayes, 1983). Moreover, attempts to initiate training measures such as YOP served only to illustrate the inadequacies of existing training provision and to legitimate the further extension of mass training as a good thing. However, at this time pragmatism and reformism also combined to enable colleges to maintain levels of student intake threatened by the collapse of local labour markets. In this respect LEAs and colleges were not 'innocent' parties in the marketplace negotiations that took place in the late 1970s, wherein the flexibility of the points system allowed cash and provision to change hands.

Thus the way in which private enterprise finds its expression in the arrangements of Further Education is not a new phenomenon. Indeed, the ethos of contemporary FE is rooted in its voluntaristic and entrepreneurial traditions, which have for long been associated with the fortunes of the local labour market. Unlike mass schooling, FE has taken a highly individualistic path, its survival depending very much on the patronage of local industry and the ability of individual colleges to attract greater student numbers. As Tipton (1973) has noted, the points system alone has ensured that many colleges remain in a perpetual state of flux, since they are constantly called upon to redefine their courses to attract new customers. Not only has this ensured that the colleges operate on the basis of market forces, but that they also seek to manipulate the points system to ensure expansion and growth. Consequently the emerging pattern of FE provision since the postwar period has been patchy and has come to depend on a points system firmly anchored to the production forecasts of local industry. Perhaps not surprisingly the development of those staple forms of provision which fall within the compass of FE have traditionally tended to be both parochial and chauvinistic, catering mainly for the needs of young male apprentice workers.

With the decline in demand for industrial craft work (manufacturing, shipbuilding, steel and so forth) in the 1960s and 1970s, FE was compelled to compensate for its loss in student intake by recruiting from a flourishing tertiary and service sector. The erratic pattern of industrial and corporate development in the 1960s, strange as it may now seem, led to demand for 'new' types of trained labour and new courses; in business and management studies, technician education, secretarial, social work, nursing, GCE studies and so forth. Thus, as a result of entrepreneurial expansion, many colleges became less tied to the fortunes of local manufacturing industry, particularly in the south-east, and could recruit from a wider intake of full and part-time students than hitherto. Yet despite the progressive appearance of FE at this time, and claims that it offered a genuine 'second chance' of social mobility for working class youth (Bristow, 1976; Cantor and Roberts, 1974), the vast majority of school leavers remained outside FE and training. According to Hordley and Lee (1970) the main beneficiaries of FE at this time were the middle class who were more likely to adopt FE as a 'second chance' (or even as a 'second choice'—Raffe, 1979) route into employment or higher education.

Thus from arguments so far it would seem that the forces which impelled expansion of FE in the 1960s and 1970s correspond more closely to shifts in the occupational structure than to any clearly thought out policy of FE and training. Consequently, it is not difficult to discern the motives underlying the diversification of FE at this time, which led to the shelving of many low status courses and the upgrading of others. Neither is it surprising that regional and other labour market conditions acted to heighten competition between the colleges, resulting in the proliferation of new courses which, ironically, rendered the FE system less open and less comprehensive than it might at first appear. It was not until the late 1970s and the early 1980s with the establishment of YOP, and later YTS, that FE was able to tap the unemployed and unemployable market made available to it via MSC funds (Gleeson and Mardle, 1980). As on previous occasions, the stimulus to broaden the FE training base arose in relation to dramatic changes in the youth labour market: in this case its almost total collapse. It is this space that the DEP and its major agent the MSC has sought to exploit in recent years and which has, somewhat paradoxically, opened up new avenues of training reform.

Since Crowther the overall failure to establish a coherent policy for 16–19s has enabled the MSC to make political capital out of existing inadequacies of provision, while at the same time manipulating the entrepreneurial legacy of FE to its own advantage. Not only has this secured the state's management of school-to-work transition as a permanent feature of social policy, but it has also redefined the relationship between FE and the labour market it once served. If such state intervention has enhanced the corporate image of FE, by redefining its curriculum toward national rather than local objectives, (Moos, 1984), it has also drawn attention to the failure of the DES, LEAs and colleges to provide post-school FE and training to the majority of school leavers. Although in its earliest days the Conservative government was suspicious, even hostile, toward an expensive quango such as the MSC, it has since recognized the MSC's ideological and tactical significance. Thus, under the aegis of enlightened reform, following on the Great Education Debate (1976–1979), the Conservative government, via the MSC, has established direct control over non-advanced FE and training and achieved a tighter grip over both the transition and transmission points between school and work. By this method central government has gained access to the education system and its resources, and encroached on decision-making territory previously occupied by the DES, LEAs and unions. This is epitomized in the recent switch in resources from the rate support grant to the MSC, in order to fund the takeover of 25 per cent of non-advanced FE work. Clearly such practice represents a distinct break with established social democratic thinking which, until the late 1970s, characterized policy- and decision-making processes in education.

If, however, the MSC is seen to have taken the initiative by extending provision to a sector of school leavers previously excluded from training policy, it remains far from clear what benefit they derive from their 'new' experience. While patterns of participation in FE and training by class, race and gender have altered in recent years, evidence suggests that the position of young people in the labour market has changed very little (Raffe, 1983; Dex, 1983; Lee and Wrench, 1984). Moreover, close inspection of student participation in various types of courses suggests that there exists a close interplay between those divisions found in the labour market and those found within FE and training itself (Gleeson *et al.*, 1983). Perhaps not surprisingly, as training opportunities have expanded in recent years, the existence of tripartite divisions have become more apparent. Though certainly less selective in intake than in the past, FE now directs its courses to three broadly defined yet distinct target groups. Elsewhere (Gleeson, 1983) I have described these as:

—the traditional though now declining male *craft* apprentice intake (now including female craft skills: typing, child care, beauty therapy, hairdressing, cookery and so forth).
—the *academic/technical* intake of the late 1960s and 1970s: including business, management and technician studies, secretarial, nursing and social work studies, GCE studies and so forth.
—the *tertiary modern intake:* the unemployed and unemployable of the 1980s; the curriculum of which is largely given over to generic skills training, work experience and 'life skills' training.

Though in practice far less discrete, such broad divisions indicate something of the patchwork nature of FE and training provision at the present time. Hence, tripartism, crude device as it may appear here, broadly reflects and delineates various changes in the youth labour market and the kind of opportunities (or not as the case may be) open to young people. Noticeably, the forms of curricular knowledge associated with the different routes not only separate off various categories of student, but they also confirm their status in the labour market hierarchy. At the level of teaching, administrative and curricular relations, for example, these distinctions are made manifest in a number of covert ways. Assessment of the academic/technical students' higher calibre is reflected both in the ways teachers perceive the commitment and motivation of such students (Gleeson, 1980; Avis, 1981) and in terms of the physical resources allocated to them. As the so-called high status element of the curriculum has grown, a tendency now exists to categorize increasing numbers of FE conscripts as 'less able', and the courses they undertake as

'Mickey Mouse'. This is noticeably the case in relation to YTS and other related low-level courses which are associated with 'remedial training' (Atkinson and Rees, 1982). In the specific case of female participation in nursing, child care and other gender-specific courses, this assumes an even more questionable dimension: here vocational training represents little more than a reinforcement of gender roles and an apprenticeship in home crafts (Blunden, 1983; Gibb, 1983). Elsewhere, evidence regarding black youth on YTS courses indicates that they are consistently more likely to be allocated to schemes offering inferior opportunities of subsequent employment (Lee and Wrench, 1984; Fenton *et al.*, 1984). The 'catch 22' for black youth is that no matter which route they take, and no matter what their level of qualifications in comparison with whites, they suffer disproportionate discrimination in the job market (Brown, 1984). This view would seem to confirm the conclusions of a recent report which indicates that 'if you had the misfortune to be born in the 1960s, and are therefore seeking your first job in the early 1980s, it does help enormously to be born the right sex and right colour, and into a family with the right occupational connections' (Lee and Wrench, 1984).

While it would be misleading to exaggerate the sort of tripartite divisions so far described, there is little doubt that State training policy for the unemployed has simply added another dimension to the existing fragmented pattern of post-school provision. Cuts in education budgets and the sequestration of rate support funds in favour of the MSC have, moreover, increased the pressure to treat the unemployed as a distinct rather than an integrated group within the broader context of FE and training. There is at present enormous pressure on the colleges and LEAs to respond to the training requirements laid down by the MSC: many face the prospect that if they are unwilling to 'service' MSC requirements the MSC will simply look elsewhere and utilize the private sector to satisfy its 'off-the-job' requirements. The problem has been affected further by changing regional and demographic factors which have intensified competition between schools, colleges and MSC for a statistically declining cohort of 16-year-olds. As the following diagram would seem to indicate, the direction of 16-year-old leavers remains as confused as ever, with noticeable divisions opening up between YTS, non YTS and full-time provision.

In the absence of any comprehensive policy to deal with such a fragmented situation, a two-tier system of provision has arisen almost by default: one half administered and controlled by the DES and LEAs, incorporating academic, technical and occupationally related forms of education and training, and the other, administered and controlled by the MSC, incorporating 'on-the-job' and 'off-the-job' forms of training. Despite resistance on the part of the colleges to such a division there are clear indications that many LEAs have surrendered a sizeable proportion of non-advanced FE work to the MSC and that others, stripped of cash, are soon likely to follow. The danger is that a significant section of non-advanced FE will simply become the 'dumping

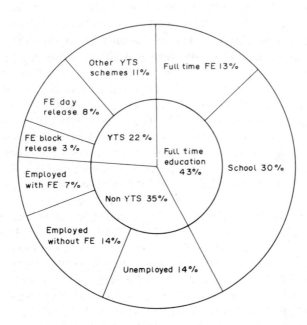

Educational and economic activity of English 16-year-olds 1983/84 (*TES,* 7 December 1984).

ground' for increasing numbers of dissident and disaffected young people (Moos, 1984). One consequence of this administrative separation is that it reinforces arbitrary divisions between education and training, and marginalizes the unemployed as a separate category with their own particular institutions, curriculum, teachers and so forth. It is to this aspect of the discussion that I now wish to turn.

## VOCATIONAL LITERACY

So far in this paper I have sought to demonstrate the ways in which state training policy has reinforced rather than challenged various tripartite divisions within Further Education and training. It has also been argued that the rise of vocationalism marks a response to certain ideological imperatives, and should not be confused with making young workers or industry more efficient. According to Moore (1983), the vocational 'realism' currently associated with the new training paradigm conceals its inherent irrationality; its purpose is seen as blocking a coherent social and political understanding of the world of work. To date, however, the curricular implications of this argument have not been seriously taken up. Perhaps understandably the dominant emphasis has been on the macro-conditions of training; the ways in which training represents a substitute for employment, a mechanism for regulating youth labour markets, and so forth. In various ways this approach has identified a number of important structural functions associated with training policy, not least in relation to the ways in which it:

—reduces the level of youth wages;
—encourages employers to train rather than employ;
—hands trainees over to employers for positive vetting;
—enacts employer definitions of worker status;
—reduces the significance of the apprenticeship system, and so forth (LRS, 1984; ILP, 1983; NTG, 1983).

Yet, despite evidence which indicates that training creates a pool of low wage workers, it is the ideological arguments in favour of how private enterprise *ought* to work that is important for understanding the essential curricular ingredients of the new vocationalism. The kinds of arguments which, for example, support generic skills training do not find their expression in work practice, but in an idealized conception of how industrial relations ought to function under free market conditions. The ideological significance of skills training is that it projects the learner as a flexible entity, capable of being employed or re-employed in a variety of different jobs within the same occupational training family. Essentially there are two problems with this notion of training for competency in OTFs. In the first place there is no clear evidence what transferable skills are, how they are transmitted and how they are transferred (Jones, 1984). Secondly, OTFs assume a causal connection to exist between work and the curriculum: the assumption being that one can unambiguously work backwards from work to the type of training required for the performance of that work. Elsewhere in Further Education, developments in business, management and technician education reflect this causal mode of curriculum design. Such a model suggests that once synchronization between technical education and work is achieved, the educational system will simply provide the type and commodity required by the labour market. It is within this idealization of the links between work and education that contemporary training policy is located: its aim is to reduce worker dependence on outmoded skills and to ensure the adaptability of the worker in the face of changing economic circumstances. Consequently, a major selling point of transferable skills training to employers is not the level of technical skills it imparts but the *type* of labour it provides. In this respect youth training takes on a different meaning from that traditionally associated with training for a specific job. Here the concept of socialized labour trained for *anything* is perhaps a more accurate assessment. Thus, despite the apparent vocational realism employed in this approach, no discernible links exist between the content of training provided and the actual content of work available. This is most marked in the area of 'self-starting', an element designed to introduce entrepreneurship into the curriculum. Whether intended or not, attempts to prepare trainees to earn a living or make out in non-work situations (by 'starting your own business' or by 'preparing for self employment') pre-set young people to think of themselves *outside* rather than within the mainstream of society. From this perspective it is not vocational realism but vocational idealism that has come to challenge contemporary educational practice (Esland and Cathcart, 1984).

If the spirit of individualism evident in such an approach bears the imprint of radical conservative thinking, it should not be confused with attempts to increase the the efficiency of industry or to enhance the freedom of the individual. Rather, it is the uncertainty of the young's employment prospects which legitimates the construction of 'skills training' and allows the state to 'protect' youth from the inimical influence of unemployment. Perhaps not surprisingly, within the context of communication and life skills training 'standing on one's own feet' is not concerned with the individual acting on society, or of him/her struggling against the forces that entrap him. Essentially, the life management approach to 'SLS' training emphasizes individual *adaptation* and *survival*: society as such is not thrown open to question other than in the narrowest of terms. Consider, for example, the MSC's view of the skills trainers are asked to evaluate under the heading the 'World Outside Employment'.

*World Outside Employment*

|  | Not yet | Yes with help | Yes |
|---|---|---|---|
| The importance of keeping clean | | | |
| How to use a bank or building society | | | |
| How to plan money | | | |
| About any staff discounts, the social club etc. | | | |
| How to be loyal to the workplace | | | |
| What people expect of each other away from work | | | |
| How to apply for a job | | | |
| How to use the telephone | | | |

(MSC, 1984)

What is perhaps most revealing here is the preface, which describes the checklist as 'a variety of skills and knowledge which when understood can assist a young person to develop within the community as a whole'. Elsewhere in the same notes of guidance 'personal effectiveness' is measured in terms of the trainees' ability to 'talk to strangers', 'be polite and helpful', 'behave in the right way', and so forth (MSC, 1984). In this respect the curriculum supporting such basic skills represents little more than a crude attempt at colonizing everyday life (Atkinson, 1984), linked with filling in forms, opening accounts and generally 'being good'. Not only does this kind of prescriptive approach fail to get to grips with the very real educational and learning difficulties which affect young people, but it also conveys an implicit assessment of their position and worth in society. One consequence of this is that trainees are made more aware of what mainstream society expects of them, in terms of attitude, behaviour, motivation and so forth, but which as *outsiders* is nevertheless beyond their reach.

Under these circumstances youth training represents little more than a particular form of mass vocational literacy which shifts responsibility for the reproduction of workers back onto themselves. Training the employed not only enables them to 'stand on their own two feet' (after all we trained them) but it also seeks to handle the perceived workers' reproduction deficiencies, i.e. their lack of basic skills. By making workers more responsible for their own destinies (epitomized in the terms 'on your bike'—Tebbitt, 1983; 'taking your skills with you'—Hayes, 1983) in this way no recriminations can be made against employers or the state, since it is the market that is the deciding factor. In this respect training policy simply replicates nineteenth-century liberal economic thinking: the point being to have an unlimited elastic supply of labour, the quality of which is not *that* important (Broady, 1981). The paradox of training is that the demand side is presently being manufactured by the state, via the MSC and its managing agents, and cheap labour 'sold back' to employers as a going concern. As the following newspaper advertisement sandwiched between second-hand cars and situations vacant indicates, YTS labour can be 'conveniently' marketed and packaged like any other product.

> Work Experience Places Wanted—No Cost to Employers. School-leavers who have been professionally trained in typing and other secretarial subjects by Sight & Sound are available for work experience with Central London employers under the Youth Training Scheme. No cost to employers, no paperwork. Please ring our YTS Liaison Officer for full details (*London Evening Standard*, 25 October 1983).

While there is, of course, no clear evidence that basic skills training has any direct effect on young people's attitudes, it is perhaps what gets left out of the curriculum that is important: notably the absence of any general and political education. Yet, somewhat ironically, recent attempts to keep politics out of training (Morrison, 1983) have only drawn attention to this neglected area: Peter Morrison's now famous proclamation that 'I am totally convinced that the youth training is all about the world of work, and I don't want it to get a bad name if politics got involved' (*TES*, 23 September 1983) has, if anything, increased public suspicion of the MSC's political ambitions in redefining curricular priorities in this area. Despite attempts to play down the censorship of political education in YTS, there can be little doubt, as the following communiqué from the MSC makes clear, that politics has little to do with learning about British Industry.

Managing agents should note that their agreement with the Commission requires that the training programme be run in a 'manner acceptable to the Commission'. A key requirement will be that it is not involved in any activity of a political nature or any activity likely to bring the Commission into public controversy or discredit. If this requirement is not met it could result in the immediate closure of a programme (from *A Handbook for Managing Agents*, 1983).

It would seem evident from such remarks that the debate about 'teacher accountability' has shifted in a direction unforeseen by the DES in the immediate years following Jim Callaghan's Ruskin Speech (1976). Despite the problem of how to teach trainees about work without reference to the wider structures of society, such directives convey an obvious political message regarding the MSC's view of training, and its own standing with employers. Perhaps this explains why the MSC has chosen to opt for 'guidance and counselling' as a more acceptable means of fostering in young people those skills which will enable them to adopt '. . . the right role at work' (MSC, 1983). Closer inspection of the meaning of this phrase indicates that 'acceptance of authority', 'taking orders' and 'work skills' represent the most significant core elements of the skills involved (MSC, 1977, 1982). Quoting from MSC guidelines, Seale (1983), for example, detects a 'semi-punitive' approach to counselling.

4.2 The role of the counsellor
He/she must be aware of
4.2.1. any change in work performance against the trainee's norm
4.2.2. signs of alienation in matters of time-keeping, discipline etc., and
4.2.3. any unsatisfactory relationships
Any of the above must be seen as a need for counselling. (MSC guidelines quoted in Seale, 1983).

Here counselling is seen by Seale as little more than a mechanism for policing the individual's motivation toward work, and providing essential information for inclusion in his/her personal profile. No less remarkable is the MSC's appraisal of the skills essential to what it terms 'a satisfactory private life' (MSC, 1977, 1982), wherein the skills of 'making friends', 'resisting provocation' and 'making conversation' represent the extent of MSC thinking on the subject.

That this is all there is to life or that such limited conceptions eschew political involvement reflects, of course, a particular ideological position which presents training as a neutral mechanism necessitated by individual rather than structural constraints. From this position questions regarding how industry is organized and managed, how wealth is accumulated, how wages, skills and allowances are legitimated and sustained, can be conveniently edited out of training as politically extraneous. The political effect, however, is to separate off the study of work from the society which surrounds it, thereby reducing the entire framework of industrial matters to a narrow set of technical propositions. As a consequence, 'learning about British industry', and 'entering the world of work' become little more than euphemisms for learning about one's place. It is within this overall structure that trainees' political horizons are controlled and their broader vision of the issues and possibilities which surround them severely restricted.


## BEYOND CRITIQUES?

It could, of course, be argued that the issues to which this paper are addressed are simply political and economic in nature, the solutions to which cannot be conceived of in terms of education and training alone. Having said this, however, the discussion of possible alternatives does not automatically follow on. It is also the case, for example, that the problem cannot be explained in terms of the truism 'there ain't no jobs', crucial as this may be. One of the ironies of MSC policy is that it has drawn attention to longstanding issues in the relationship between school and work, which predate the rapid increase in unemployment in the late 1970s. Prior to this time little sociological interest was taken in the fate of young workers entering dead end jobs, the majority of whom had little or no access to further education or training. If the research literature and official documents in this period focused on topics such as 'occupational choice' and 'career opportunities', the reality open to many young people was that of low paid and unskilled work. Thus to simply demand a return to the full employment conditions of the sixties, even if that were possible, ignores the limiting effects of various types of work on young people's long-term social opportunities. As Roberts (1984) has recently argued, popular as a mass extension of unskilled or semi-skilled work might appear at the present time, it would not alleviate the problem of low pay, boredom and chronic job changing: neither would it clarify what the relationship should be between education, training and work. The problem at the moment is that chronic job changing has been replaced by chronic scheme changing (Raffe, 1983) without any fundamental appraisal being made of the nature of work itself.

According to Tipton (1983), there is a basic flaw in much of the current thinking about how to improve the quality of training; its terms are that no questions are asked about the quality of work, its structure, design, organization and so forth. At present, extending training for existing forms of monotonous and humdrum work is likely to increase conflict and tension between trainees, teachers and employers as expectations are frustrated. To date, the nature of work has been taken as given by educationists and others and, as a consequence, few attempts exist to combine policies for training with policies for work design. Moreover, trade unions and employers have shown little interest in the need for workers to participate in well-designed jobs or even reduce working hours. Yet, as Tipton (1983) argues, training *is* for jobs. The likelihood is that little will be achieved on this front until a legal duty is placed on employers to consult with unions on all training issues, and the right to education and training is placed on the collective bargaining agenda. Despite the obvious pitfalls, only by redefining and restructuring work patterns does it offer the possibility that 'training for work' may take on a broader meaning than the present narrow vocationalism allows. Little will happen on this front until trade unions are more actively involved in industrial democracy (Bullock, 1977) and government and industry legally obliged to cooperate in matters regarding work design, training and the further education of all workers. Without such cooperation it is unlikely that training provision in its present form will inspire much confidence or public support.

This, however, is likely to pale into insignificance if both an educational policy and an enlightened funding programme for 16–18-year-olds is not found which will address the present patchwork nature of non-advanced FE provision. At the root of the problem is a totally inadequate system of financial provision for students in this age group: at the moment their lack of political muscle renders them prey to parental dependence, discretionary grants or the MSC's 'shilling'. While the situation of such students is unlikely to stir so much as a backbench revolt, the sheer size of the problem suggests that jerry-built training will, in the long term, not succeed. Given that increasing numbers of school leavers are unlikely to enter the labour market much before eighteen or nineteen, the arguments for building a comprehensive education and training system are compelling (TUC, Labour Party, 1984); not least because the ground rules of schooling have significantly changed. Regional, demographic, occupational and other factors have not only altered the structural relationship between school and work but they have also called into question present makeshift arrangements for regulating young people's entry to the labour market. To date there has been no concerted attempt to develop a coordinated education and training policy for the 16–19 age group as a whole. Instead we have witnessed a succession of critiques of standards in education and the assumed failure of teachers to direct pupils toward more vocationally relevant subjects. Meanwhile the traditional examination system has remained untouched other than in terms of tinkering with the GCE/CSE system and introducing an array of 16+, 17+ and other pre-vocational reforms. As such the 'new' vocationalism has followed a separate path from mainstream schooling and has done little to challenge entrenched assumptions regarding high status knowledge in the curriculum and its close association with the examination system and the labour market hierarchy. In this respect the dominant emphasis on theoretical, abstract and scientific knowledge has gone largely unquestioned by the MSC. For the so-called disadvantaged, however, the dominant pedagogic experience has been extended and remains firmly anchored within practical, relevant and vocational knowledge: a form of control traditionally associated with ensuring the lower orders obligation to the system and their awareness of its dominant moral codes.

Perhaps the major weakness of contemporary training policy is that it neither specifies specific skills training nor provides an adequate general education. Thus, under present conditions, the young lose out both ways: on the one hand they do not gain marketable or recognized skills and, on the other, they do not acquire knowledge and understanding, however broadly defined, which allow them critical insight into the political or economic workings of society. Perhaps not surprisingly, the expansion of vocational training has resulted in inferior general education, without the employment prospects of young people altering much one way or the other. One effect of YTS, and also TVEI, is that it forces young people to settle on vocational training and employment issues too early on. Despite the publicity given to core areas and transferable skills training, early specialization narrows the options open to young people later on in life. Consequently, without a broadly based general education it is most unlikely that students will be able to utilize forms of training which they have not been educated to absorb.

Unpopular as the demand for general education may be at present, the indications are that employers, educationists and others do not recognize the validity of contemporary skills training, which is not seen to embody the general indicators of competence required to gain access to the job market. It is perhaps time to recognize that experimentation with generic skills training has been a failure, and that the sacrifice of general education for a gain in vocationalism has not been worth the trade (Jackson, 1981). The perfunctory time accorded to learning either technical 'know how' or acquiring general knowledge suggests that students are getting neither education nor training. The irony, as Willis (1984) has pointed out, is that working class youth who know much about work, and are prepared to put up with its most boring and exploited forms, should have basic work skills pushed down their throats from a very early age. Moreover, the fact that so few workers eventually end up in trades for which they were trained suggests that training without general education has, anyway, little vocational relevance. The likelihood is that a broadly based education, which combines learning about work alongside the study of society, including options drawn from the arts, sciences, humanities, social sciences and so forth, will in the long run have more public support and perhaps possess greater vocational relevance. This is not to advocate resurrecting piecemeal injections of liberal studies or political education which, in the sixties and seventies, were driven like a wedge into the curriculum to offset the worst effects of over-specialization. What is called for at the present time is a balanced curriculum which integrates a broad range of theoretical and practical skills, and which seeks to break down existing tripartite divisions. Bringing education back in will not be an easy task, not least because the terms and conditions of conventional liberal humanist education have changed. As Tipton (1983) has argued, if educationalists and teachers feel understandably squeamish about becoming involved in 'narrow' training, then the solution is to reconstitute the debate surrounding the relationship between education, training and work. Perhaps the major starting point here is to define vocational education and training more broadly, to emphasize the active involvement rather than separation of youth from mainstream society, and to treat their needs as seriously as those of employers. As one commentator has recently noted, it is not dole schools or work experience that the young unemployed require now but 'schools and' (in a well-known phrase) 'really useful education and rewarding, unexploitative work' (Horne, 1983). If, in the short term, jobs are not available to 16–18-year-olds they should not be fobbed off with 'cottage industry' employment (handyman repairs, gardening, delivering, housework, helping the aged and so forth) or compensated for their loss with remedial schemes that do little more than infantalize them and make them even more dependent on the State. It is this aspect rather than unemployment itself which perhaps constitutes the present 'crisis', and which poses as much an education as an economic problem. The obvious need at present is to consider programmes for education and training alongside a programme for jobs. Education and training without the possibility of employment as a foreseeable goal is not only politically unacceptable but it is likely to cast doubt, no matter what the quality, on various types of training provided (Roberts, 1984). What is required now are *policies* which do not simply delay entry into work or provide employers with cheap labour (this only exacerbates unemployment) but policies which offer young people systematic career development, training and opportunities for full-time skilled work (Casson, 1979). It is a contribution to this aspect of the present debate about education and training that this paper is addressed.

## REFERENCES

Atkinson, P. and Rees, T. (eds.) (1982) *Youth Unemployment and State Intervention*, Routledge & Kegan Paul, London.

Atkinson, P. (1984) Interruption and reproduction: the classification and framing of work and education. Paper presented at the SSRC/CEDEFOP Conference on 'The transition between school and work', Berlin, January 1984.

Avis, J. (1981) Social and technical relations: the case of Further Education, *British Journal of Sociology of Education*, 2, 2.

Bates, I. *et al.* (1984) *Schooling for the Dole*, Macmillan, London.

Baxter, J.L. and McCormick, M. (1984) Seventy per cent of our future: the education, training and employment of young people, *National Westminster Bank Quarterly Review*, Autumn.

Blunden, G. (1983) Typing in the Tech, in Gleeson, D. (ed.) (1983) *Youth Training and the Search for Work*, Routledge & Kegan Paul, London.

Bristow, A.J. (1976) *Inside the College of Further Education*, HMSO, London.

Broady, D. (1981) Critique of the economy of education, in *Economy and Industrial Democracy*, 2, 2.

Brown, C. (1984) *Black and White Britain*, PSI.

Bullock, A. (Chairman) (1971) *Report of the Committee of Inquiry on Industrial Democracy*, CMND 6709, HMSO, London.

Cantor, L. and Roberts, I. (1974) *Further Education in England and Wales*, Routledge & Kegan Paul, London.

Casson, M. (1979) *Youth Unemployment*, Macmillan, London.

Crowther Report (1959) *15–18*. Central Advisory Council for Education, HMSO, London.

Dex, S. (1983) Second chances? Further education, ethnic minorities and labour markets, in Gleeson, D. (ed.) (1983) op. cit.

Esland, G. and Cathcart, H. (1984) The compliant creature worker: Paper presented at the SSRC/CEDEFOP Conference on 'The transition between school and work', Berlin, January 1984.

Fairley, J. and Grahl, J. (1983) Conservative training policy and the alternatives, *Socialist and Economic Review*, Autumn.

Fenton, I. *et al.* (1984) *Ethnic Minorities and the YTS*, MSC, London.

Gibb, V. (1983) The recreation and perpetuation of the secretarial myth, in Gleeson, D. (ed.) (1983), op. cit.

Gleeson, D. (1980) Streaming at work and college, *Sociological Review*, November.

Gleeson, D. and Mardle, G. (1980) *Further Education or Training?* Routledge & Kegan Paul, London.

Gleeson, D. (ed.) (1983) *Youth Training and the Search for Work*, Routledge & Kegan Paul, London.

Hayes, C. (1983) Taking your skills with you, *TES*, 20 May 1983.

Hordley, I. and Lee, D.J. (1970) The alternative route: social change and opportunity in technical education, *Sociology*, **4**.

Horne, J. (1983) Youth unemployment programmes, an historical account of the development of dole colleges, in Gleeson, D. (ed.) (1983), op. cit.

ILP (1983) *The Tories' Poisoned Apple*, Independent Labour Publications, Leeds.

Jackson, P. (1981) Secondary schooling for the poor, *Daedalus*, no. 4, Fall.

Jones, P. (1984) *What Opportunities for Youth?* Youthaid Occasional Papers, No. 4, London.

Lee, G. and Wrench, J. (1984) 16–18: The crisis of the school leaver, *Universities Quarterly*, Autumn.

LRS (1983) *Youth Training: A Negotiator's Guide*, Labour Research Dept., London.

Moore, R. (1983) Further education, pedagogy and production, in Gleeson, D. (ed.) (1983), op. cit.

Moos, M. (1983) How far further for further education? *Youth Policy*, 2, 1.

Morrison, P. (1983) Report of a BBC Radio 4 Interview, by Jackson, M. (1983) 'Forces rally against political ban', *TES*, 23 September 1983.

MSC (1977) *Instructional Guide to Social and Life Skills*, MSC, London.

MSC (1981) *A New Training Initiative: Task Group Report*, MSC, London.

MSC (1982) *Guidelines on Content and Standards in YTS*, MSC, London.

MSC (1983) *A Handbook for Managing Agents in YTS*, MSC, London.

MSC (1984) *Notes of Guidance. Occupational Training Families*, (Bowyer and Sanzen), June 1984, MSC, London.

NTG (1983) *Training and the State: Responses to the MSC*, Network Training Group, Manchester.

Raffe, D. (1979) The alternative route reconsidered, *Sociology*, **13**.

Raffe, D. (1983) Education and unemployment, in Gleeson, D. (ed.) (1983), op. cit.

Roberts, K. (1984) *School Leavers and their Prospects*, Open University Press.

Robinson, E. (1968) *The New Polytechnics*, Penguin, Harmondsworth.

Ryan, P. (1984) The New Training Initiative after two years, *Lloyds Bank Review*, No. 152, April.

Seale, C. (1983) FEU and MSC: two curricular philosophies and their implications for YTS. Unpublished mimeo, Garnett College of Higher Education, London.

Tipton, B. (1973) *Conflict and Change in a Technical College*, Hutchinson, London.

Tipton, B. (1983) The quality of training and the design of work, in Gleeson, D. (ed.) (1983) op. cit.

TUC/Labour Party (1984) *A Plan for Training*, TUC/Labour Party Liaison Committee, London.

Venables, E. (1967) *The Young Worker at College: A study of a local tech.*, Faber & Faber, London.

Watts, A. (1983) Schools and the YTS, *TES*, 13 May 1983.

White Paper (1984) *Training for Jobs*, HMSO, London.

Willis, P. (1984) Conclusion: theory and practice, in Bates, I. *et al.* (1984) op. cit.

# 5

# Trends and Structural Changes in English Vocational Education

## MICHAEL FARLEY

To date, Britain has been unique amongst the major industrial European countries in the extent of its neglect of the majority of its young people as they move from school to adult life. Throughout the twentieth century, Britain has given priority mainly to those young people who remain in full-time education, entering higher education thereafter usually to take academic degree courses. It has largely failed to meet the needs of young people who leave school at the minimum leaving age. Of course, there has been some part-time education and training for the relatively few young people in apprenticeships, but the vast majority of school-leavers have thereafter received no systematic preparation for adult life whatsoever.

In 1959 the Crowther Report recommended full-time education to 16 and part-time education to 18. Whilst the former was implemented 13 years later, no government has chosen to introduce a right to part-time education up to the age of 18. The issue of day release was taken up again in 1964 with the publication of the Henniker-Heaton Report which modestly recommended a 'doubling' over five years in the numbers of young people being day-released from employment for further education; that represented an average annual increase of the order of 50,000 for five years. Henniker-Heaton was never implemented. It appeared at a time when all the resources were concentrated on the Government's crash programme to implement the Robbins Report. But in addition to its unfortunate timing, it had major flaws. First, it was merely concerned with the technical education of those already possessing prescribed qualifications and it ignored the pressing needs of the majority. Second, it rejected the principle of compulsory day release as laid down in the

Source: From Watson, K. (ed.) (1983) *Youth, Education and Employment*, Croom Helm, London.

ETE–F

1944 Act and reaffirmed by the Crowther Report. The inadequacy of response to the Report was reflected in an actual fall in take-up of day release. Thus it has not been the case that resources have been unavailable: quite bluntly successive governments preferred other policies. Throughout the 1960s and 1970s resources were used to expand higher education—without incidentally any significant increase in the proportion of working class students entering universities—whilst almost nothing was done to strengthen post-school provision for the vast majority who receive no opportunity of any kind for further education or training. And on top of class inequalities, girls continue to fare worse than boys, blacks continue to fare worse than whites, the disabled do badly, and there are regional disparities as well.

## INDUSTRIAL TRAINING LEGISLATION

Alongside this neglect of the vast majority of young school leavers, has rested a tradition of 'voluntarism' in respect of skill training. That Britain has a lower proportion of its workforce formally trained than any other comparable European Community (see Table 1) country reflects this tradition which is characterized by non-intervention by government in vocational education and training. Britain, for example, is one of the few advanced industrialized countries where apprenticeships are not regulated by law and in which no qualifications are required by law, for example, to set up as a builder or to start a car repair shop.

Vocational education and training has been dominated by the perceptions of individual employers and the bargaining aims of those trade unions which represent exclusive groups of highly skilled workers. Most of all there has been for many years a tradition that individuals advanced in vocational careers through their own initiative and personal effort, often studying part-time, frequently in the evening, and generally with little or no assistance from either government or employer.

In the early 1960s there arose a more general acceptance that such attitudes resulted in arrangements that were insufficient in both quality and quantity, and after a brief attempt at stimulating industry by offering the help of a joint employer/trade union body, the Industrial Training Act became law in the same month as the Henniker-Heaton Report appeared. The Act was of great historical importance since it recognized that industrial training could no longer be left to the voluntary arrangements of employers. Its objective was to ensure an adequate supply of properly trained men and women at all levels of industry and commerce; to secure an improvement in the quality and efficiency of training; and to share the cost more evenly between employers.

The Act set up twenty-four industrial training boards (ITBs) with responsibility for training in each industry and for financing certain industries' training needs through a levy on the firms within the industry.

*Table 1*

| Column | 1 | 2 | 3 | 4 | 5 | 6 |
|---|---|---|---|---|---|---|
| Country | Full-time general education | Full-time vocational education | Apprenticeship | Work for unemployment | Other & unknown | Total % |
| Belgium | 55 | 36 | 4 | 4 | 1 | 100 |
| Denmark | 23 | 13 | 30 | 31 | 3 | 100 |
| W. Germany | 21 | 19 | 50 | 9 | 1 | 100 |
| France | 27 | 40 | 14 | 19 | – | 100 |
| Ireland | 56 | 10 | 5 | 29 | – | 100 |
| Italy | 20 | 50 | 4 | 23 | 3 | 100 |
| Luxembourg | 31 | 31 | 23 | 15 | – | 100 |
| Netherlands | 35 | 29 | 9 | 26 | 1 | 100 |
| Great Britain | 32 | 10 | 14 | 44 | – | 100 |

Source: European Commission.

The Act also improved the machinery of industrial training but its stick-and-carrot approach required firms to pay a levy—not to train—although by not doing so they forfeited a training grant. While the ITBs have improved the education and training of young people at craft level, there remains little done to meet the needs of young people in semi-skilled and unskilled jobs.

There was rapid dissatisfaction with the 1964 Act which centred around six main criticisms:

—criticism from employers, especially smaller firms, about the financial sanctions of the ITBs;

—criticism about the bureaucratic behaviour of the ITBs;

—lack of progress in avoiding shortages of skilled labour;

—inadequate co-ordination of training in occupations and skills which were not confined to one industrial sector;

—absence of national manpower policies;

—inadequate progress towards meeting the needs of young people in semi-skilled and unskilled jobs

Consequently, in 1973, the Employment and Training Act set out to restructure substantially the vocational training mechanisms. It created a new body, the Manpower Services Commission (MSC), which was formally set up in 1974, with the intent of bringing together all the main mechanisms within the labour market. The establishment of the MSC marked an important step in linking training with other labour market activities. At the same time it unified, administratively, training services aimed at companies and other employing bodies, with training services aimed at individuals who are unemployed or who want to improve their employment opportunities by acquiring additional skills.

It was the setting up of the MSC which was to have major implications for young people in their transition from school to adult life. For as youth unemployment has risen alarmingly the MSC has become massively involved in running programmes for the young unemployed, and indeed the adult unemployed, through its Special Programmes Division (SPD). In addition, as governments have paid increasing, albeit still modest, attention to the needs of those young people who leave school at 16 and who enter jobs where hitherto they have received little or no systematic continuing education or training, the MSC, through its Training Services Division (TSD), has become substantially involved in this area of activity.

Such is the involvement of the MSC in matters of interest and concern to the education service, that in 1976 a Training and Further Education Consultative Group (TFECG) was established. This provides a national forum for discussing matters of common interest to the training and education services and seeks to promote collaboration between the MSC, the ITBs and industry more generally, on the one hand, and the diverse organizations in the education service (LEAs; Regional Advisory Councils;

examining bodies; teacher organizations) on the other. It has to be recorded, however, that the Group has had only a very limited impact on policy decisions and on relationships between the training and educational worlds. Members of the Group cannot—and were not expected to—commit the major representative organizations in the education service or industry to policies or views advocated by the Group. It has therefore inevitably become something of a 'talking shop', and, without executive or policy responsibilities, unable to exercise much influence or initiate much purposeful activity.

Nevertheless, there was, and remains, a need for a consultative body which brings together authoritative viewpoints on issues of concern among the various 'constituencies' within the education and training services, and consideration of its future is currently taking place.

## MSC INVOLVEMENT WITH YOUNG PEOPLE

*Unified Vocational Preparation (UVP)*

In July 1976 the then Labour Government published a statement entitled *Unified Vocational Preparation: a Pilot Approach* which proposed a limited programme of experimental schemes of vocational preparation for those young people who left school and entered jobs where hitherto they received little or no systematic continuing education or training. The Unified Vocational Preparation (UVP) pilot programme embodied two basic essentials: firstly, that the education and training services be jointly responsible for planning and providing vocational preparation and that its education and training elements be inseparably combined; and secondly, that the provision made should be focused on the working situation and be seen by employers and the young people concerned as relevant to their needs.

The July 1976 statement identified the potential target group for UVP as some 300,000 per annum, although in 1979 the Training Services Division of the MSC estimated that the total size of the potential UVP target population was nearer 200,000. Originally a total of twenty schemes was planned for the academic year 1976–77, but at the end of the three years of initial pilot programmes it was intended that the schemes would cater for up to 6000 young people per year.

The majority of schemes were launched by the Distributive Industry Training Board and the Rubber and Plastics Processing ITB. Other Boards involved included the Food, Drink and Tobacco ITB and the Paper and Paper Products ITB. A substantial number of schemes were launched by colleges of further education. The National Foundation for Educational Research carried out a two-year independent evaluation of the programme between 1977 and 1979. This evaluation is reported in the NFER's publication *Unified Vocation Preparation: an evaluation of the pilot programme* (Wray, Moor and Hill, 1980).

It is worth recording the benefits of UVP felt by employers and trainees.

(a)  By employers:

—more flexible and better trained workforce, more adaptable trainees;
—improved timekeeping, productivity and industrial relations;
—lower turnover, reduced absenteeism of young employees;
—increased motivation and commitment;
—positive and earlier identification of trainees' potential;
—improved relationships with educational bodies, including colleges.

(b)  By trainees:

—more self-confidence and self-esteem;
—greater sense of involvement and achievement;
—enjoyment of education, often for the first time;
—improved knowledge of company, products, markets and self;
—better citizen, more competent adult;
—increased interpersonal skills and capacity to work in a team.

The initial pilot programme was subsequently extended until July 1981 and in November 1980 the intention to further extend and expand schemes of UVP was announced. This expansion was to involve about 10 per cent of the identified target group (that is, about 20,000 young people). A subsequent announcement indicated a further expansion to a target of some 50,000 places by 1984–5.

## The Youth Opportunities Programme

The Youth Opportunities Programme (YOP) was proposed in the MSC report *Young People and Work* (May 1977) (MSC, 1977) which was drawn up by a working group chaired by the present (1982) director of the MSC, Geoffrey Holland. It was essentially a response to the increase in youth unemployment caused by international recession and public expenditure cuts.

The Programme was to provide unemployed young people under the age of 19 with training and work experience appropriate to their individual needs and to help each individual young person secure a permanent job at the earliest possible moment. In view of the rapidly escalating rate of youth unemployment the government has had to expand YOP rapidly.

Each YOP scheme is intended to offer the opportunity for young people to:

—acquire knowledge and skills relevant to employment;
—practise those skills within the context of real employment;
—be supported and advised by a responsible adult.

Each scheme is intended to be self-contained and can include both structured training and work experience. Where appropriate, young people can, if they fail to find employment at the end of one scheme, progress to another that offers enhanced opportunities for training and/or experience. Young people can continue in YOP up to one year through a sequence of schemes.

The MSC itself provides very few opportunities within the Programme directly. The vast majority of entrants go into places provided by sponsors who are private employers (63 per cent), local authorities and other public bodies (26 per cent) or voluntary organizations (10 per cent). There is no compulsion on young people to participate in the programme. They are paid by the MSC through their sponsors. The young people are MSC trainees and not the sponsor's employees. Places are notified to the careers service and employment service who advise individual young people on the opportunities that will best meet their individual needs. In most cases, a number of unemployed young people will be submitted to any particular opportunity within the programme and a sponsor is entitled to accept or reject candidates.

At local levels, the programme is planned and supervised by twenty-eight area boards who are also responsible for approving applications from those who wish to run schemes, projects or training courses. The area boards are supported by the regional and area offices of the Special Programmes Division of MSC. At national level, the Special Programmes Division exercises general oversight of YOP and advises the Manpower Services Commission on policy and development.

There has been increasing and justified criticism of YOP. The main points of criticism are:

—rising unemployment for YOP leavers;
—inadequacy of training/further education on many schemes;
—job-substitution;
—the apparent lack of any positive effort to promote equality of opportunity;
—a failure to meet adequately any special needs of unemployed blacks;
—the lack of progression and integration within and from schemes;
—the inadequacy of the training allowance;
—the lack of a representative structure for the young people themselves.

Partly as a result of these criticisms it was announced by the Government in the House of Commons on 21 November 1980 that the emphasis in the Programme would, increasingly, be on working towards the point where every 16- and 17-year-old not in education or a job would be assured of vocational preparation lasting as necessary up to his or her 18th birthday and that this development of YOP would be seen in the wider context of improving preparation for, and training in, work of all young people, and not just the unemployed. In 1982/83, YOP will provide for some 630,000 entrants, of whom 100,000 will be taking part in year-long schemes.

Taken together, UVP and YOP undoubtedly have the potential to be developed in tandem into initially a twelve-month, and thereafter a two-year, programme of vocational preparation available to every 16–18-year-old wishing to take advantage of it.

## Support for skill training

The MSC, working with industry, supports a number of young people—in 1982/83 some 35,000—undertaking apprentice or other forms of long-term skill training.

## INDUSTRIAL TRAINING DEVELOPMENTS

The MSC established a policy of reviewing periodically the effectiveness with which it discharges its principal functions and in early 1979 established a Review Body to examine 'the working of the Employment and Training Act' of 1973 so far as it relates to arrangements for the promotion of training for employment, together with the provision of further education closely associated with industrial training, and the links between them, and to recommend how those arrangements should be altered or developed for the future, having particular regard to:

  (i) the future needs of the economy for trained manpower of all kinds;
 (ii) the needs of workers, including young people entering employment;
(iii) the efficient working of the labour market nationally and locally;
(iv) the need to ensure the economical and effective use of public funds.

Its Report, *Outlook on Training*, was published in July 1980 (MSC, 1980). It took the view that public policy towards training should concentrate on:
(a) ensuring there is an effective training contribution to the profitable exploitation of new technology, increased productivity, and faster economic growth;
(b) extending vocational preparation for young people;
(c) increasing opportunities for adults to enter skilled occupations, or to update or upgrade their skills through retraining;
(d) introducing efficient training methods more widely, and ensuring that appropriate standards are set and attained.

Whilst accepting that a better approach to local and cross-sector needs could, and must, be devised, the Review Body nevertheless took the view that the existing statutory framework, within which the MSC can work in collaboration with industry training bodies, could be satisfactorily developed and adapted to meet changing needs.

The Review Body's recommendation that the funding of ITB's operating costs should be returned to industry rather than continuing to be funded by the MSC caused the representatives of industry on the Review Body to reserve their position.

Despite the Review Body's view that the existing statutory framework should remain, and although the MSC informed the Conservative Government in October 1981 that its view was that no ITB should be abolished, the Government announced in November 1981 that it intended to abolish sixteen ITBs, reduce the scope of a further two, and not to meet ITB operating costs beyond March 1982. This decision infuriated the trade union movement and educational interests, both of which were actively and positively involved in the work of the Boards. The abolition of statutory ITBs is unlikely to be at all helpful in the achievement of the public policy objectives set out in *Outlook on Training*, and, in respect of young people, it will jeopardize the achievement of the UVP target.

## DEVELOPMENTS IN FULL-TIME EDUCATION

Alongside the developments for young people who leave school at 16, the education service makes provision for young people who wish to further their full-time education beyond the age of 16 but who are neither suited to academic courses such as GCE A level nor sufficiently committed to a particular occupation to embark on a course of vocational training. This is the group for whom the term 'the new sixth form' was coined, although since many of them actually transfer to further education the nomenclature Young Stayers On—YSO (to go with YOP and UVP)—is to be preferred.

Until the early 1970s, YSOs were few in number and very often found themselves on totally inappropriate courses such as GCE O level, where success was difficult. O level does, of course, enjoy an established and widespread reputation. It is the qualification which enables entry at a basic level to a number of professions. It is widely recognized and sought by employers, and parents are often anxious for their children at least to be allowed to attempt it. But as schools and colleges have started to admit a much wider proportion of the ability range at 16, the shortcomings of O level (which is intended to examine only the top 20 per cent) for this group have become increasingly apparent.

In 1972 the Schools Council published its Working Paper 45 (Schools Council 1972) concerned with the 16 to 19 age group, in which it argued the need for an additional examination for those sixth-formers who were not suited to A level work or who did not intend to remain for two years in the sixth form. Working Paper 46 (Schools Council 1973) which followed in 1973, contained the Council's initial proposals for an examination to be called the Certificate of Extended Education, which would meet the needs of these sixth-formers. During 1976, after three years of experimental examinations carried out on the lines proposed in the Working Papers, the Schools Council formally recommended that the CEE be established and recognized nationally. However, the then Labour Government eventually set up a committee to consider the CEE proposals and in April 1978 the Keohane Committee was appointed. In December 1979 the Committee's report was presented in Parliament by the new Conservative Government's Secretary of State for Education and Science, Mark Carlisle. Unfortunately the CEE was a single subject examination with no vocational bias and was not therefore very popular with the new government.

In 1973 as a result of requests from schools and colleges for courses with a vocational orientation for students in full-time education, the City and Guilds of the London Institute made detailed inquiries into the needs of students in post-16 education. Their findings indicated that, although the existing pattern of courses was suitable for many students there was a large group of students whose precise needs were not being catered for. The Institute carried out a series of feasibility studies in 1974 to attempt to define these needs more clearly and to investigate ways of meeting them. In the academic year 1976/77, the City and Guilds 'Foundation Courses', the product of the previous year's feasibility studies, came into operation and became generally available to schools and colleges. Unlike CEE, Foundation Courses have a complete, integrated curriculum with some vocational orientation.

Pilot schemes in the Certificate of Further Education were first introduced in 1974 by the Regional Examining Bodies which were then responsible for technical education. They were devised initially for the same target group as CEE, but provided a more vocationally-oriented course.

In addition to these developments the Business Education Council and the Royal Society of Arts offer (separately) courses such as the General Diploma and the Vocational Preparation (Clerical) Course for young people with few, if any, academic qualifications who wish to enter, or have already entered, employment in industry and commerce, distribution and the public sector. Despite these national initiatives there are a considerable number of institutions that are faced with students whom they feel can only adequately be catered for by an internally-designed course. Some of the courses developed by individual schools and colleges make limited use of external examinations; others lead to the award of an internal certificate, and some are not certificated at all. They also vary considerably in their degree of vocational emphasis. At one end of the spectrum are pre-vocational courses which, in common with CFE courses, raise students' attainment to a level where they can progress to more conventional vocational training and/or employment in a specific field and at the other, general educational courses whose aim is primarily to improve students' literacy and numeracy skills. Courses are often the result of a desire to cater for minority groups in the locality, particularly recent immigrants but also physically handicapped youngsters or those from ESN schools, so that the content of certain courses reflects the particular needs of these groups.

Over the past decade there has, therefore, grown up a provision of courses for YSOs which is both confused and confusing. In an attempt towards rationalization, the Further Education Curriculum Review and Development Unit (FEU) established a Study Group to consider the range of full-time pre-employment courses available in England and Wales for young people over the age of 16 who wish to stay on in further education usually for a year without, initially, any specific vocational or academic commitment.

Its report, *A Basis for Choice* (ABC),[6] (DES, 1979) suggested a curricular framework which would introduce some cohesion into existing provision and at the same time allow for local initiatives.

The Government considered both the Keohane Report and *A Basis for Choice*, and, subsequently in a consultative paper, effectively rejected CEE in favour of provision broadly along the lines of ABC. Government proposals for a new pre-vocational qualification at 17+, the Certificate of Pre-Vocational Education (CPVE), were finally published on 20 May 1982. This Government White Paper states that courses leading to the CPVE should:

—offer a broad programme of general education with emphasis on the practical application in various types of employment;
—develop personal attributes such as self-motivation, adaptability, self-reliance, a sense of responsibility and an ability to work constructively with others;
—help each student to discover what kind of job he or she might expect to tackle with success.

Part of each course, says the paper, should be common to all students. It should include written and spoken English, mathematics, aspects of science and technology and their application in the modern world, studies designed to give a broad understanding of citizenship and its responsibilities, the way the country earns its living and the nature of its institutions. Careers education and guidance should be provided throughout the courses. The paper's emphasis is on assessment and certification. It rejects norm-referenced examining as being inappropriate.

The paper suggests that the relevant examining/validating bodies undertake the administration of the CPVE as a joint enterprise in the form of a small consortium under an independent chairman appointed by the Secretaries of State. The local authority associations would also be represented on the consortium.

Currently there is much discussion taking place on the practicability of the suggested consortium approach, and it is known that BEC and CGLI have jointly put forward an alternative suggestion to the Government. Should disagreement over the management of the CPVE, however critical it may be, lead to any further delay in its introduction (due in September 1984) serious damage will be inflicted on the education service.

The FEU followed up its publication of ABC with a number of other documents. All of these recognized that the present unique combination of demographic trends, new technology and recession must result in irreversible changes in our attitudes to work and education; that many current generalizations regarding work, education and employment are breaking down; and that any curriculum formula for post-school education and training will have to take these things into account. In particular it will have to take account of:

—the development needs of adolescents;
—changing and uncertain patterns of work;
—the realization that the formal education system is not the sole agency in the education/training process;
—the need to solve local problems with local solutions.

Had *A Basis for Choice* not been published when it was, a curriculum document having many of its characteristics was probably inevitable because there is currently an inflexible and restrictive vocational training/education system; an examination system that has an emphasis on penalizing error rather than rewarding success; a tendency to specialize as early as possible and thus neglect broad-based and transferable skills; a tendency to undervalue non-intellectual skills and experiential learning; a tendency to regard counselling, guidance and negotiation in education and training as optional extras; an inequality of provision and financial support in many parts of our education/training systems.

The FEU document, *Vocational Preparation* (DES, 1981), emerged from these aspects of actual or desirable change. Much of that which is said in Vocational Preparation by the FEU has a great deal of congruence with criteria laid down in a European dimension.

The lessons for the education service post-school in all this can be summed up very simply: *it has to be willing to work with others and it has to appraise its own practices.* This reappraisal will mean the following in post-school education:

1. It must give as much attention to experiential and non-academic learning as to conventional academic knowledge.
2. It must learn to design educational programmes in consultation with other people, not least with the young people themselves.
3. It must accept that 'low-level' work in academic terms should rank more highly in esteem, seniority of post and in resource provision.
4. It should regard counselling and reflection as essential to the teaching of knowledge and skills.
5. It should regard assessment as a counselling opportunity.
6. It must realize that the formal education system is only one element of

education. Other agencies have equal expertise and, sometimes, additional facilities.

The approach to UVP, YOP and YSO provision outlined in the FEU's publication *Vocational Preparation* has received near universal acceptance throughout the education service. It argues that the main aims of vocational preparation are:

(a) to give young people basic skills, experience and knowledge;
(b) to help them assess their potential, to think realistically about jobs and employment prospects and to optimize their employability;
(c) to develop their understanding of the working and social environment, both nationally and locally, so that they may understand the variety of roles possible for them to play as an adult member of society;
(d) to encourage them to become progressively responsible for their own personal development.

Vocational preparation is, thus, a combination of education and training designed both to assist the smooth transition from school to work, and to support a young person in the early stages of working life. The content and aims of vocational preparation are derived as much from the perceived needs of the young people themselves as from a predetermined range of disciplines; and the schemes accordingly demand an integrated approach to the planning of content. Its aims range more widely than those of many conventional courses; its content necessarily spans a wide range of disciplines, and a variety of strategies have been adopted to provide the type of learning which gives vocational preparation its distinctive characteristics.

## THE NEW TRAINING INITIATIVE

Taking up the recommendations of the Review Body which examined the working of the 1973 Employment and Training Act, the MSC published in May 1981 a major Consultative Document *A New Training Initiative* (NTI) (MSC, 1981a). This proposed three major objectives for the nation. These were:

(i) to develop skill training including apprenticeship in such a way as to enable young people entering at different ages and with different educational attainments to acquire agreed standards of skill appropriate to the jobs available and to provide them with a basis for progression through further learning;
(ii) to move towards a position where all young people under the age of 18 have the opportunity either of continuing in full-time education or of entering a period of planned work experience combined with work-related training and education;

(iii) to open up widespread opportunities for adults, whether employed, unemployed or returning to work, to acquire, increase or update their skills and knowledge during the course of their working lives.

A parallel consultative document on the 'Open Tech' dealt with the potential of open learning systems for enhancing training opportunities for adults.

The NTI Consultative Document argued that the nature of the technological changes now being implemented throughout the world, the emergence of the newly industrialized countries, the redistribution of manufacturing capacity worldwide all mean that Britain has entered a period of rapid and far-reaching transition.

It pointed out that the effects can be seen clearly in what has been happening to jobs. Those jobs that require very limited skills have been disappearing rapidly: 600,000 were lost between 1971 and 1978, and even more will disappear in the next five years. Blue collar jobs are fewer; white collar jobs will outnumber them by 1985. There has been a sharp falling away in the numbers of traditional craft jobs and a marked increase in demand for technicians and technologists. Employment in manufacturing has fallen and jobs in the service sectors have increased. All these changes will continue into the future.

The new markets and technologies require a more highly skilled, better educated and more mobile workforce in which a much larger number of professional and technical staff are supported by a range of more or less highly trained workers who perform a range of tasks and who are involved in a process rather than the repetitive assembly or manufacture of a part of a specific product.

Both firms and individual people are having difficulty adapting. Young people face special difficulties. Apprenticeship, traditionally the heartland of Britain's training provision, proved to be increasingly inadequate to present and future needs. Youth unemployment continues to rise alarmingly. At school young people have often been less well prepared than they should be for working life. The vocational relevance of much that they have been taught has not been made clear to them. On leaving school opportunities to gain comprehensive training have been limited to the relatively small number of occupations, including apprenticeships, for which this is customary.

The consultative document attracted considerable public interest. Nearly 1000 written responses were received from employers, trade unions, local authorities, educational representatives and others. There was widespread agreement about the Commission's analysis of the training problems faced, and of the objectives set out in the Commission's consultative document. While there were, not surprisingly, differences of view and emphasis about ways of moving ahead, there was almost unanimous agreement on the need for urgent action. With that in mind, the Commission set out in its report *A*

*New Training Initiative: An Agenda for Action* (MSC, 1981b), published in December 1981, a number of specific proposals for action to implement each of the three key objectives.

At the same time, the Government itself published a White Paper setting out its proposals for immediate and longer term action directed to achieving the objectives of NTI. This contained many proposals which drew on the Commission's recommendations in *Agenda for Action*. The White Paper also announced the Government's intention to ask the Commission to establish a new youth training scheme to replace the existing Youth Opportunities Programme and to guarantee from September 1983 a full year's training for all unemployed 16-year-old school-leavers in the year after they leave school and to make provision for unemployed 17-year-old school-leavers but without the same guarantee. In a full year the scheme would provide over 300,000 places at a total cost in 1984/85 of over £1 billion. For the financial year 1982/83, however, the Government envisaged providing resources for some 100,000 year-long training opportunities within YOP as an interim objective pending the realization of the more ambitious plans for a youth training scheme.

While on many matters the recommendations in *Agenda for Action* were mirrored in the proposals of the Government's White Paper, on others—for example, the allowances for young people proposed by the Government and their eligibility for supplementary benefit—the White Paper proposals were at variance with the MSC's approach.

These and other issues were examined by a Youth Task Group subsequently established by the MSC in January 1982 which was asked to devise and recommend a comprehensive scheme of vocational preparation for all young people under the age of 18 not in full-time education, whether in work or not. Such a scheme was to contrast with and would, it was hoped, replace the Government's White Paper proposal for a Youth Training Scheme, which not only concentrated almost solely on 16+ unemployed school-leavers, but also proposed lower allowances and the withdrawal of supplementary benefit rights. Represented on the Group were the CBI, the TUC, the Local Authority Association, the Youth Affairs Lobby, the Careers Service, voluntary organizations and professional education interests.

There was some urgency to the Group's work. The Government's Scheme was to begin in September 1983 and whatever transpired would require a considerable lead time (at least a year) for planning and development prior to its implementation. Consequently the Group met frequently, and on occasions at length, during February, March and April, finally producing a unanimous Report, which was approved by the MSC on 27 April 1982. The full Report was published in early May, and the Government, after much hesitation and many threats, finally accepted the Youth Task Group's proposals.

The Group's main proposals in respect of a Youth Training Scheme (YTS) are that:

1. Training will be provided for all 16-year-old school leavers and those 17-year-olds leaving full-time education who become unemployed within the first year of leaving. The scheme will cover 400,000 16-year-olds and 60,000 17-year-olds in 1983–84.
2. The programme will be designed to provide twelve months' training but this will be flexible depending on circumstances.
3. Young people on the scheme will receive an allowance which is exempt from income tax and national insurance. The Task Group recommended that this should be £25 per week and should maintain its real value. This means about £28 per week in September 1983. Supplementary benefit entitlement is not to be affected, so there will be no financial disincentive for those who choose not to join the scheme.
4. The majority of places will be provided by employers, but as under YOP, voluntary organizations and others will be able to act as sponsors of schemes such as Community Projects or Training Workshops.
5. Like YOP, the new programme will be administered and funded by the MSC, advised by a national supervisory board. Any organization that wishes to act as a sponsor will need to be approved by the local board of the MSC. Approval will depend upon a capacity to contribute to the objectives of the scheme and conformity to overall guidelines and policies established by the MSC. The hope is that some organizations would take on the role of managing agencies and would organize the contribution of a number of individual organizations in any particular locality.

In June 1982 the Commission issued a further Consultative Document reviewing the local machinery for the delivery of YTS. The consultative period ended at the beginning of September 1982.

YTS would appear, therefore, to take on board the second objective of NTI. What of the first, which also related to young people? This, the development of initial skill training, including apprenticeships, is being examined by a group of MSC officials whose first report was before MSC Commissioners at their July 1982 meeting. This report suggests that the aims should be to secure:

(a) entry into skill training free of age barriers; genuinely open to a wide range of recruits (not least, girls); and free of unnecessary academic requirements.
(b) skill training processes free of time-serving and organized on a modular basis.
(c) standards of attainment, with associated modules and tests, for all key occupations in the engineering, construction, road transport, clerical and commercial, and computer fields.

It also considers exactly how apprenticeship and other similar arrangements might come within the scope of the Youth Training Scheme, noting that the Youth Task Group assumed that first-year apprentices would eventually come within YTS and that there would be further selective support for skill training beyond this.

Thus, the report rejects a two-tier approach in which a minority of school leavers enter skill training, while the majority (who currently receive little or no training) would enter YTS, in favour of a more comprehensive approach under which all school leavers enter YTS. This is absolutely right, despite some major problems which will ensue. One is that YTS provides for only three months off-the-job training as compared with up to the whole year for many current first year apprenticeships. Nevertheless, the inclusion of the first year apprenticeship within YTS will surely hasten desirable reform and lead to the development of apprenticeship training on a modular basis which could then also apply to skill training for adults.

## THE PRESENT STATE

There are, now, therefore, two distinct providers seeking to meet the needs of young people in Britain in transition. On the one hand, the education service, traditionally providing for those who remain in full-time education: on the other, the MSC providing for the rest. Each currently has three threads, although those three provided through the MSC are to come together within YTS (see Table 2).

*Table 2*

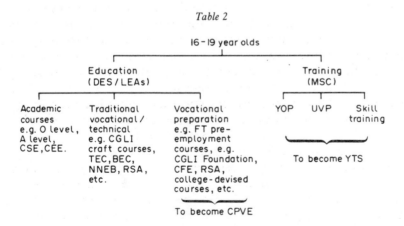

There are in addition a number of young people on supplementary benefit who study part-time and a number who continue to require basic education to enhance employment and life prospects (such as those with special educational needs).

It is not only the source of provision which differs. The financial arrangements between education and training differ. Training provision through the MSC is funded centrally, albeit channelled through local mechanisms. This gives central government control. Education provision is funded locally albeit with some central input. This gives local government some control. These differences raise issues of accountability and local input. MSC provision automatically attracts an allowance (in the case of YOP) or a wage. Provision made through the education services does not, and rarely, if ever, does a young person who remains in full-time education enjoy adequate financial support. Without a substantial improvement in the financial income of those in the age group who continue in education, some young people will undoubtedly be attracted away from full-time education for the wrong reasons. This likelihood will increase when CPVE and YTS are properly developed and common objectives are covered by the same syllabus.

And for young people, it has long been the view of many, including the FEU and the National Association of Teachers in Further and Higher Education (NATFHE) that UVP, YOP and YSO—and now YTS and CPVE—should be seen as but different modes of vocational preparation. It is, therefore, crucial not only that YTS and CPVE permit movement from one to the other, but also that they become integrated into other arrangements for the age group.

If they do not, young people are not going to be able to move smoothly to and from education, training and work as appropriate. The construction of such bridges and ladders demands accreditation of schemes within YTS. It is worth stressing that accreditation in this context does not mean some sort of pass/fail concept—that would be anathema—but rather that each young person should be given a profile of assessment and experience that can be shown to employers and education and training providers. Only with such accreditation will barriers to transfer be eliminated. (Such an approach would also have a beneficial 'spin-off' effect in assisting the marketing thrust.)

If barriers are not eliminated a new, dangerous and alarming variant of the 'two nation' theory will emerge. This danger is ever present since, although a great deal of initial hostility between education and the MSC has diminished, considerable suspicions still remain on both sides.

These suspicions will not easily be erased and could even increase. Should, for example, the MSC establish its intended national group of professionals with expertise in initial training, vocational preparation, standards and scheme design for young people who have left full time education to advise its national supervisory board without an adequate involvement of the education service; should it go ahead with its proposals to develop a small but effective field force to act as inspectors without first gaining the co-operation of the education service and of Her Majesty's Inspectorate; and should it persist with its apparent intent to establish local delivery machinery without it having proper representation from professional education interests, then education will rightly be both suspicious and aggrieved. But if the MSC makes a conscious attempt to use existing facilities and expertise, and not set out to re-invent the wheel, and if it sets out to ensure that the design-base of YTS allows young people to move easily from YTS to CPVE and vice-versa, then good-will and co-operation will undoubtedly flourish. But there is still a tendency to guard jealously what are seen as important sectional interests.

For its part the education service must recognize the distinctive differences between vocational preparation (sometimes, correctly, referred to as the 'new FE') and traditional education provision. The latter in its vocational form within further education (FE) has, as its crucial influence, the claimed requirements of certain occupations, industries or professions for which the young people concerned are being prepared (in the case of full-time courses), or have already entered (in the case of part-time courses). Within these parameters, FE has undoubtedly been flexible and responsive to change in such things as employment patterns and job specific skills. Nevertheless, in the final analysis, traditional vocational courses within colleges, including TEC and BEC courses, have their curricula defined by claimed job requirements and, in large measure, their students determined by previous attainment and job choice. The same is true of academic provision where the curriculum is largely defined by the demands of higher education and students defined by their previous cognitive attainments. There is one further factor of relevance to the categorization of traditional education: the dominance of, and the students' dependence on, the teacher. None of this is meant to be disparaging, for traditional education has and will continue to serve the more able and fortunate of young people—and their parents and employers—exceedingly well.

But vocational preparation cannot have its curriculum defined by the demands of higher education or of an assumed destination simply because neither of these sources apply. Nor will its students be determined on the basis of their previous attainments. So inevitably there are distinctive differences between vocational preparation and more traditional provision, and these differences demand a distinctly new approach to both curricula and pedagogy.

The service will also have to come to accept that vocational preparation programmes can be provided on an inter-agency basis and that, very often, the background against which effective learning takes place is the working and adult world so that approaches need to be based on experience which is as direct as possible. Education also has to appreciate that co-operation with other agencies is not a sign of incompetence but a sign of professional maturity.

One thing is certain, neither the interests of young people nor those of the nation will be served should the education and training interests fail to co-operate enthusiastically at all levels.

## A TERTIARY SYSTEM

The evolution of a tertiary (post-16) sector for all young people, heralded by the developments of YTS and CPVE, will be accelerated by the inevitable disappearance of the traditional school sixth-form, at least in its present institutional form. This inevitability is the result of demographic decline which is rapidly making the present organization of sixth form provision in schools unviable, economically as well as educationally. Already many LEAs are finding that the only way in which 11–18 or 13–18 schools can be maintained is by closures and/or amalgamations, which are not popular either with parents, or with other local people. Another solution sometimes considered, that of sixth-form consortia between schools, is never likely to be anything other than a temporary one, and is, in any case, unpopular with young people. Nor will many new separate sixth-form colleges be established, and those that now exist are likely to develop into tertiary institutions. In terms of comprehensiveness, administrative convenience, educational effectiveness and excellence, as well as the efficient use of resources, such a tertiary development makes greatest sense.

Moreover, the development of a tertiary system of post-school education will make the evolution of an undivided education and training system, at least for young people in transition, easier to achieve. And such an undivided tertiary system would enable the starting position in respect of provision for the age group to be the needs of each and every individual young person him/herself.

The objectives of such tertiary provision would then become:

(a) to ensure a full range of full-time courses for the entire post-16 age group;
(b) to ensure appropriate general, pre-vocational or vocational education for the entire community, including all young workers and the young unemployed;
(c) to make special arrangements for those with special needs;
(d) to act as an *ad hoc* agency for the training needs of business, industry and other organizations;
(e) to ensure formal leisure opportunities for the whole community;
(f) to act as an agency for the promotion of sporting, recreational, cultural and educational activities;
(g) to develop beneficial activities not falling into the above categories.

## THE FUTURE

The CPVE and YTS proposals hold the potential for a major advance, an important step on the road towards comprehensive provision of training and educational opportunities for all young people between the ages of 16 and 18, including those hitherto scandalously neglected. That potential could yet be thwarted. There is a contradiction at the heart of much Government thinking. It wishes the focus to be on training for *employment*, yet the engine of change and the force that releases Government resources is massive and ever rising youth *unemployment*. This contradiction has led a number of local trade unionists, educationalists and youth workers to dismiss YTS as little more than a device for keeping young people out of the unemployment figures. Moreover, the Government has by its enthusiasm for destroying most of the statutory ITBs apparently signalled its belief that education and training and retraining for adult life is of minor consequence. Worse, its policies at the Department of Education and Science—CPVE apart and belatedly—hardly exhibit a concern for young people at all.

Of course, there remain substantial issues to be resolved. Will CPVE get off the ground? Will a real partnership between education and training develop? What criteria will be used to determine quality within YTS schemes? And who will be involved? How compatible will YTS be, not only with CPVE, but also with the rest of the education and training system? What interests are to be represented on the various bodies concerned with delivery? What role will the education service play at the local level? How is the crucial issue of staff development to be tackled? Will the young people themselves be interested? How much of the intended three months off-the-job training and/or relevant further education will be provided by the education service? Will there be sufficient sponsors? Will the education service have, or be provided with, the necessary accommodation, equipment and staffing? How accountable will local and national machinery be? Will traditional forms of provision accept the challenge and undertake the alterations needed? And, the biggest question of all, will resourcing be adequate, for CPVE and YTS, and for young people themselves?

The unanimity on YTS so far achieved and maintained amongst all interested parties within the MSC has, at times, appeared fragile. There can, however, be few illusions about the task ahead if every young person between the ages of 16 and 18 is to be offered initially a 12-month programme, and subsequently a two-year programme, of high quality vocational preparation with national accreditation.

But with high quality, proper delivery and adequate resourcing, the prospect is of a major advance in provision for young people who have until now been disgracefully neglected. This advance has long been an aspiration justified by the arguments of emancipation and justice. It is now also a basic social, economic and technological necessity.

YTS and CPVE are only the beginning of establishing satisfactory vocational preparation arrangements capable of meeting the needs of all young people in the 1980s and 1990s as they make the transition to adult and working life. But their potential should be embraced and moulded towards a tertiary concept of comprehensive, unified and continuing education and training provision for the entire age group.

# REFERENCES

Department of Education and Science (1979) *A Basis for Choice.* Further Education Curriculum
   Review and Development Unit, Stanmore, p. 22.
Department of Education and Science (1981) *Vocational Preparation.* Further Education
   Curriculum Review and Development Unit, Stanmore.
Manpower Services Commission (1977) *Young People and Work,* London.
Manpower Services Commission (1980) *Outlook on Training,* London.
Manpower Services Commission (1981a) *A New Training Initiative: a consultative document,*
   London.
Manpower Services Commission (1981b) *A New Training Initiative—an agenda for action,*
   London.
Schools Council (1972) *16–19: Growth and Response 1: Curricular Bases,* Working Paper 45,
   London.
Schools Council (1973) *16–19: Growth and Response 2: Examinations Structure,* Working Paper
   46, London.
Wray, M.J., Moor, C. and Hill, S. (1980) *Unified Vocational Preparation: an evaluation of the
   pilot programme,* Windsor, National Foundation for Educational Research in England and
   Wales.

# 6

# Gender Divisions, Training and the State

ANN WICKHAM

## INTRODUCTION

The post-war period in Britain has seen increasing state intervention in the area of training, especially with the establishment and subsequent growth of the Manpower Services Commission. However, successive governments have shaped training provision differently, especially the most recent Conservative Party administration with its neo-Liberal commitment to the Free Market. Yet throughout the changes to be seen over the last thirty years, one thing has remained constant, the subordinate position of women within the training process. Although there have often been reports and policy statements which point to the disadvantaged position of women on the labour market and the importance of training provision in helping to transform this situation, commitment appears to have remained very much at the formal level. Little or nothing has been done to transform the situation in practice as far as central government agencies are concerned.

The exclusion of women from many training opportunities is not just an oversight or explainable by reference to a lack of interest by women whose central concerns are thought to be the home and family. Instead many feminists now argue that it is in male interests to continue to exclude women from 'masculinized' jobs and confine them to the female ghettoes of low-level, low-paid, jobs in feminized work sectors, thus producing the sex segregated patterns of employment with which we are all familiar.

A recent paper recognizes that men organize to exclude women from certain jobs, struggle with women over entry to certain occupations, and that

Source: A revised and extended version of an article published in Whitelegg, Elizabeth (ed.) (1982) *The Changing Experience of Women*, Martin Robertson, Oxford, pp. 147–163.

the presence of women in some jobs has materially damaged men's chances. Such conflict could be put down to 'false consciousness' and to not seeing that capital is the real enemy. But in fact material advantages accrue to men from women's disadvantaged position at work.[1]

The authors also comment on men's control over technology and the question of skill. In both cases these are elements which are the outcome of class struggle but also of gender struggle. Work skills, especially in relation to industry, have traditionally been seen in terms of craft skills and craft workers have almost overwhelmingly been male workers. While the concept of skill can refer to technical competences, it can also cover more subjective judgements, elements that workers or unions can use to defend themselves against other employers or workers.[2] In this context the assets which women bring to their work have been persistently devalued. As Phillips and Taylor[3] note, skilled work has become almost by definition that work which women do not do. This definition of skill is seldom challenged although, as Pollert emphasizes in a study of female tobacco workers:

> The irony comes when a system of co-called non-discriminatory 'objective' job 'measure-ment', aimed at getting rid of the awkward 'interference' of ideological judgements, succeeds in rooting them more deeply.... One might legitimately inquire why such a job as hand stemming (in practice, female) in Group A should be rated lower than security patrols (in practice, male) in Group D. One job might hold more responsibility and danger but the other involves more patience and physical discomfort.[4]

In other words, the definition of a skill is socially constructed and whilst the concept of 'skilled work' may be used by working-class men for their own benefit in maintaining privileges in relation to employers, it can also be used against women whose work, once defined as low skilled, is also low paid. These practices help reinforce subjective perceptions of women's marginal place in the labour market and their dependence in the home.

Training is traditionally seen as the means through which skills can be acquired and the apprenticeship system is at the basis of this approach. In the post-war period more and more training schemes have been introduced at different levels and for different periods of time, culminating in the present youth training programmes of the Manpower Services Commission (MSC). Such schemes are presumed to pass on those technical skills which the economy requires. However, in many cases it seems clear that training involves the acquisition of social attributes required in the labour process —work discipline, for instance—just as much as technical skills. When women have no access to training it effectively excludes them from many occupations, whether it is technical or social skills that are required, or even if training qualifications are being used solely as a form of entry requirement without reference to their content. Undoubtedly the absence of schemes for women is important when women want to enter what have been male-dominated occupations. However, it is essential not to overemphasize the impact of training. One must realize that even if women replicated the training available to men it is unlikely that they would gain an equal place on the labour market given the existence of competition from males, and when they are faced by male-dominated unions, male employers and a capitalist system that has profited from the use of women as a marginal, low-paid labour force.

Despite this, the extension of training opportunities to women could be of benefit to some and their entrance into less marginal areas of economic activity could help weaken the dominance of the belief that the place of women is in the home.

## EARLY DEVELOPMENTS

For much of the post-war period little attention was paid to the training of women workers. In the pre-war period, state involvement in training in general was minimal. After the First World War instructional factories were set up for ex-servicemen. In the 1920s training centres were used to deal with unemployment and in the Second World War they were used to provide rapid training for hurriedly mobilized workers. In the fifties, however, there was even a decline in the number of such training places and the main concern expressed in government circles was for apprentices, that is mainly male workers.[5] However, labour shortages, technological changes and a 'baby boom' prompted more wide-ranging considerations which were embodied in the assumption that 'upskilling' (the need to increase the skills of the workforce) was essential for economic growth.

In 1956 a sub-committee was set up under the Ministry of Labour which produced the Carr Report, *Training for Skill*[6] in 1958. In this report, which was concerned with the adequacy of the training of young workers for industry, only one short section dealt with opportunities for girls. It was assumed in the report that girls would marry and therefore would not need training. The main concern expressed was for the above average female grammar school pupil who might be expected to make a sustained contribution to the labour force. In this the Report both reflected much of the current thinking about women in other areas of social policy and anticipated the relative neglect of women's training over the next decade.

In terms of school education, for instance, the Crowther Report[7] published in 1959 (the year after the Carr Report) also assumed that the main interest of girls was in their future role of wives and mothers. Similarly, the Newsom Report[8] in 1963 concentrated upon marriage as the more important vocational concern of girls, despite mounting evidence of the importance of women workers within the economy.

The emphasis upon marriage and the notion of the dependence of the woman upon the male wage-earner which was implicit in so many areas of British welfare state policy[9] reduced the pressure for any further training provision for women even when, as in the Crowther Report, the paucity of women's day release opportunities was specifically commented upon. Curricular differentiation in the schools both taught girls that their main interests were in the home and closed them off from many of those training opportunities which existed. The clustering of girls in arts subjects is well known,[10] yet various apprenticeships and forms of training often require a maths or science qualification. Thus even when girls did enter further education and training, it was likely to be in areas defined as 'female', such as secretarial work or nursery nursing.

Whilst many government reports and the whole thrust of the welfare system emphasized the place of women in the home, the development of training opportunities for women would remain a rhetorical commitment. When changes were initiated in the 1960s and the government started to introduce training legislation, the issue of provision for women was still not regarded as one of importance. In 1964 an Industrial Training Bill[11] was brought into Parliament which marked a revolution in state thinking in relation to training. Until then, training had mainly been left to the efforts of individual firms. However, this *ad hoc* process was now considered inadequate, especially in the face of overseas industrial competition. Industrial Training Boards were to be set up which would help establish an overall training policy and oversee its implementation. A levy system was to spread the cost across industry. Yet in the debate around this Bill, the problem was conceptualized in almost exclusively male terms and the absence of reference to the numbers of women entering employment was publicly noted.[12] The dominance of human capital theory in this period reinforced this emphasis on men. Education and training were regarded as an investment which would later produce calculable returns. However, only men were regarded as producing economic returns. The benefit of any investment in women was regarded as social and not economic.[13]. This approach both legitimated and reinforced women's perceived marginality in the world of work and their role in the home.

## STATE POLICY TOWARDS THE TRAINING OF WOMEN IN THE SEVENTIES

The Industrial Training Bill, which set up training boards, reflected a commitment by the state to positive intervention in the field of training and the levy system gave a financial leverage on firms. However, as the training boards were mainly concentrated in those industries which had few women workers, their establishment did not help many women.[14] Furthermore, it was apparent to observers that the boards did not consider it their role to encourage the training of women and girls.[15] Commercial and clerical training which might have suited women were resisted by employers.[16]

In their failure to identify and come to terms with the specific training needs of women, the training boards reflected the opposition of employers and unions to women's training as well as social constraints. The TUC had issued a charter of aims for women workers as early as 1963 in which the need for the development of training for women was emphasized. In 1972 the TUC was still pressing for the development of training, on the grounds that the impact of the Industrial Training Bill had been negligible. Representatives of the TUC argued that when levy grants were made to firms the boards should insist that a proportion of the training places went to women and that special grants should be made for 'non-traditional' training and for training for those returning to work.[17] Yet at the same time many of the prevailing assumptions about the training of women were also evident in statements of the TUC representatives. These statements, in fact, often contradicted stated TUC goals. For instance, the Expenditure Committee on the Employment of Women noted that:

> The unconscious acceptance of traditional roles and occupations is well illustrated by the TUC evidence which, while favouring equal training opportunities for women, describes 'the vast majority of courses' at Government Training Centres as 'clearly appropriate only for men'.[18]

However, it was not that the courses were only suitable for men but that only men were admitted to them. The fact that the majority of places were for the engineering and construction industries was seen as the 'natural' reason for the bias towards male students. However, the unions were not the only ones to show some ambivalence towards the employment and training of women. The National Council of Women gave evidence to the Expenditure Committee that:

> ... a spokesman from the Department of Employment has recently suggested to one of our members that (a) many girls do not want training, (b) the overall employment position should be considered before training more married women; and that (c) it may not be good for the community that married women should be trained, and that the only circumstances in which more women will be trained is when there is economic need.[19]

Women were doing badly in many areas of training. In 1970 only 110 females were apprenticed to the skilled craft occupations compared to 112,000 males and less than one-fifth of those on day-release courses were female. Where girls were in apprenticeships the majority of these were in hairdressing. This situation is clearly related to the kinds of attitudes displayed by the unions and the Department of Employment.

However, further changes in training policy were introduced at the beginning of the seventies which appeared to offer some means of altering this situation. Whilst no specific mention of women's needs were made in either the Green Paper[20] of 1972 or the White Paper[21] of 1973, the Employment and Training Act (1973) initiated developments which were to have relevance for women.

The Act provided for the setting up of the Manpower Services Commission which was to manage public employment and training services through two executive arms, the Employment Services Division and the Training Services Division. The Training Services Division was to be responsible for the Training Opportunities Scheme (TOPS) which was replacing the old vocational training schemes in government training centres. Furthermore, section two of the Act which enumerated the functions of the Commission made special mention of arrangements that could be made to encourage increases in the opportunities available to women and girls.

The Training Services Division made the first important gesture towards a consideration of the special needs for women in the training process. The government had already argued that the introduction of legislation on equal opportunities for women could be expected to be beneficial in this area. In connection with the Equal Pay Act, it had agreed to remove male-female differences in training allowances. The government did not, however, propose to deal with other issues such as the distance of training centres or the absence of childcare facilities which might well have hindered the training of women. Yet the government was prepared to consider some experimental part-time training courses, even if these were only in the female-dominated commercial and clerical fields.[22]

In 1976 the Training Services Division brought out a report on 'Training Opportunities for Women'.[23] This was a result of a decision by the Commission in 1975, the year of the Equal Pay and Sex Discrimination Acts, that women were one of the groups whose training needs should be treated as a priority of special national importance. The Sex Discrimination Act[24] in fact, had gone a long way towards encouraging more and wider training facilities for women by specifically exempting certain forms of training provision from the terms of the Act. Section 47 allowed for positive discrimination in the provision of training courses for men or for women where the number of persons of that sex in the jobs that the training scheme provided for had been extremely small in the previous year. It also allowed for schemes in particular areas. Section 47 also dealt with the needs of those returning to work after a period of domestic responsibility and permitted both special training schemes and discrimination in selection for training programmes.

The report of the Training Services Division, issued against this background, recognized the inadequacy of existing training provision for women in every aspect, from day-release and apprenticeship to government training schemes.[25] It also admitted that there was an unsatisfied demand for training, and argued that there were legislative, economic and social justifications for the provision of training for women. However, whilst the report must be welcomed as the first major initiative by the state in the post-war period to consider the specific training needs of women, it gives the impression of a lack of dynamism and of a failure to develop a commitment to positive intervention. The emphasis in the report is on research into ways of assisting women and the exploration of possible ways of extending training.

The lack of dynamism in training policy is understandable in terms of the deepening economic crisis in Britain. Training provision had made no great progress in the late 1960s even though there had been open encouragement to women to enter the labour market. In the 1970s policy statements had been made in favour of women's opportunities but these were seldom put into practice as economic problems grew.

## THE PROVISION OF TRAINING OPPORTUNITIES
## FOR WOMEN

The full impact of this lack of commitment is evident in the provisions the MSC made for women. When set up, the Training Services Division was made responsible for the Training Opportunities Scheme (TOPS). The programmes in this scheme were not aimed at school leavers but at those who had been out of permanent education for more than two years, and were aged at least 19. The TOPS programmes offered a wide variety of courses from higher level programmes in management, science and technology to craft courses and provision for the commercial and clerical sectors. Both men and women were eligible for TOPS courses and the number of women on the programme gradually increased. In 1972, before the Manpower Services Commission took over, only 6000 women trained on the TOPS programme.[26] By 1975 the numbers had increased to 27,000; in 1977 the figure reached 40,881 and the figure was the same in 1978. By then women made up around 43 per cent of those completing TOPS courses and the percentage in 1980 was around 45 per cent.[27] In terms of encouraging numbers of women to train, it is clear that MSC programmes had considerable success. Unfortunately whilst the numbers of women involved increased, the schemes did not represent a change in the range or level of opportunities open to women.[28]

Women on TOPS schemes were found mainly in 'female' occupations. Most of them took courses in clerical work, shorthand and typing and they made up the majority on courses concerned with education, office machines, food preparation, hairdressing, cleaning, etc. Very few women were to be found in the higher level courses or in the government skill centres where subjects such as engineering, vehicle repair, carpentry and joinery, capstan setting machining and bricklaying were taught. (In 1978 only 658 women were on such courses in skill centres compared to 23,357 men, and women on these courses made up only 1.5 per cent of the women taking TOPS courses that year.[29]

Although the actual numbers in these courses may have increased slightly over the years, the overall expansion of TOPS courses meant that women represented no greater proportion of the overall student number.

Even though the numbers of women on TOPS schemes appear to have grown so rapidly, albeit in female-dominated occupations, there were still many other drawbacks associated with the schemes. The failure to provide childcare facilities and the fact that there were virtually no part-time training opportunities was a major hindrance. The small training allowance paid to women who also had to pay for childcare was another limitation. The small numbers of women entering courses for areas of work dominated by men has been partly blamed on the limited guidance offered by those administering the schemes[30] and the need for effective occupational guidance was continually stressed by those examining this area of work preparation.[31]

A special development in the TOPS programme has been the introduction of Wider Opportunities for Women (WOW) courses in colleges. These courses are designed, administered and financed by the Training Services Division, and aimed at women who are likely to enter manual or skilled employment. Even though participants can be 19 on entry, the courses have tended to attract older women. The courses are short and are meant to help women formulate realistic re-entry plans for work, as well as providing the information and self-confidence that will help them carry these out. Welcome as such courses are because of their particular concern for the older woman worker, it is clear that the numbers at present attending them are infinitesimal. Even more important, so far as discrimination faced by women on the labour market is concerned, is the fact that an evaluation of pilot courses found that the courses were not leading women to enter into a wider range of jobs.[32]

There is some provision of similar courses for women outside the MSC. New Opportunities for Women (NOW) courses or similar 'return to work' courses are to be found in many further education colleges. These too are mainly concerned with women returning to work after a break and they do not demand any entry qualifications. The courses vary a great deal in content, emphasis and duration. Indeed there is no clear information on how many such courses are available in Britain.

The Industrial Training Boards were also empowered by the Sex Discrimination Act to run positive discrimination and return to work schemes. However, many of these twenty-four Training Boards have now been closed down by the Conservative Government, leaving only seven Training boards in existence. MSC scrutiny and control has increased and finance has been changed. Some of the boards, like the Engineering Industry Training Board, have set up initiatives to try and improve the position of women in their sector but such initiatives tend to focus on school-leavers rather than older women and deal with very small numbers.[33] It is clear that, despite verbal commitment to the training needs of women, a commitment fuelled by government equality legislation, very little has so far been achieved in practice by state training bodies. This situation would be bad enough in a period of rising employment for all groups. In the current context it presents a gloomy picture. As current unemployment figures rise, many women are being thrown out of work and there has been a more rapid rise in their rate of unemployment than there has been for men.[34] Men's and women's jobs are segregated both vertically and horizontally in such a way that women are found primarily in the lower paid, lower level jobs and in female-dominated sectors of the economy.

Further opportunities for training at least offer some women the chance to move into male-dominated occupations where there are still employment opportunities or open paths to promotion. Training for women could also help prevent the further 'masculinization' of new occupations that are opening up. This is an important issue when it is expected that current female occupations will be hardest hit by new technology.[35] It seems clear, however, that many of the training programmes that recognize women's problems are being set up outside the MSC, although often drawing on sources of state financial assistance. Finance through the Inner City Partnership scheme can be used, for instance, to help establish training courses for women that are part-time and provide nursery facilities, both of which are essential for women with children. Such schemes are most often the ones that aim to open up opportunities in previously male dominated areas of work.[36]

The opening up of training opportunities to women in this way merely juggles numbers within an existing work pattern where the majority of women workers provide a cheap source of labour. If women were to enter male-dominated occupations in large numbers, it seems likely that these could become 'feminized occupations' with associated problems of low pay and status. Women would not necessarily make any major gains in the long term.

The possibility of more radical gains for women comes from an area of state training policy that is highly controversial and which is not aimed solely at women. It is the area of youth policy.

## THE DEVELOPMENT OF YOUTH PROGRAMMES

The youth programmes of the MSC developed from the Holland Report, *Young People and Work* which was published in 1977.[37] This Report marked the start of new developments inside the MSC which have had a major impact on the forms and sites of training offered to young people in Britain. The report was particularly concerned with the phenomenon of rising youth unemployment[38] and led to the establishment of a third agency inside the MSC, the Special Programmes Division which was set up in 1978. The Holland Report described previous efforts to deal with the unemployed in the 16-18-year-old age group as 'piecemeal and ad hoc', involving a variety of uncoordinated agencies.[39] The view of the committee responsible for the Report was that youth unemployment could be expected to rise as a result of demographic trends until at least 1981. The numbers of young unemployed were expanding rapidly, especially amongst girls, and as well the duration of unemployment was increasing. The report proposed a new and coherent programme to help this group find permanent jobs.

Two kinds of opportunities were to be offered to young trainees, work experience schemes and preparation for work courses. Many of the latter were to be offered in Further Education Colleges and consisted of assessment, short industrial and remedial courses. This marked the intervention of the Department of Employment into the specifically educational area since the MSC bought its courses in the colleges. At the same time the development of the courses marked a revolution in the concept of training itself and in what constituted the skills which training courses were to pass on.

The courses were seen by the MSC as a bridge between school and work, a period of transition which had to be situated outside of a school system which so many pupils rejected by leaving as early as possible.[40] The courses were meant to provide those 'skills' which many school leavers were felt to lack and which employers were assumed to require. In the past the notion of skill had been associated with craft work, with a combination of mental and physical dexterity in a particular area of work. Under the aegis of the Special Programmes Division a much wider definition of skill came into use. Skill was regarded more as a way of organizing activity and involved a combination of what are now regarded as individual skills and general skills, that is numeracy, communication and practical skills, together with social and life skills, attitudes to work and a knowledge of working life.[41] Training was, in this respect, given a new meaning which was removed from that traditionally used and evoked in the earlier MSC Reports.

The development of MSC programmes dealing with youth unemployment came against a more general background of political concern with the process of transition from school to work that was part of a redefinition of educational objectives under the Labour government. This in turn was part of wider concern for economic and social problems. James Callaghan's speech[42] at Oxford in October 1976 had expressed concern about the links between education and the economy. The new political priority expressed there generated a number of consultative papers[43] and initiatives which are still continuing in the 1980s. This concern was not merely British but found expression throughout the European Communities at this period.[44]

The focus on the problems created by 'youth' meant that schemes concentrating on this issue made provision for females as well as males. Widespread action in this area of training could not be seen entirely in male terms, especially as in many areas it was the young women who were suffering most from the effects of unemployment.

In 1979 a report was published on the opportunities for women and girls in the special programmes in the MSC. This report's special concern was with the ways in which women could be introduced into 'non-traditional' areas of work. The report started from the assumption that 'there are practically no jobs which cannot be done by girls, given the opportunity and appropriate training'.[45] It also recognized the specific form of disadvantages suffered by the female work force. These included a lack of confidence to enter new areas and the problem of having different educational experiences. The report thought that girls' lack of technical and mathematical skills could be directly compensated for. Stress was placed on the need to avoid reinforcing female patterns of work in the courses, work experience and temporary schemes by making use of the exemptions allowed by the Sex Discrimination Act. The problems of older women with domestic responsibilities were also acknowledged. However, once again practice failed to match up to stated policy. The Youth Opportunities Programme (YOP) offered work experience schemes and work preparation courses. In the first year there were 162,000 participants in the scheme.[46] In 1981 around 500,000 took part. This represented a rise from one in ten school-leavers to one in two. Female school leavers made up 50 per cent of those participating in YOPs and maintained this percentage despite the rise in the absolute numbers involved. However, within the programmes the same dispiriting pattern of work opportunities for women was to be found. Far more girls for instance, went into community work experience schemes, a continuation of women's role in 'caring' areas,[47] whilst more boys entered the training workshops. Work experience places in employers' premises made up the majority of opportunities in the YOPs programme and here the tendency was for further reinforcement of occupational segregation. To some extent the MSC could claim that this was out of their control, for the Commission had to rely on the voluntary co-operation of employers. Employers, particularly in small firms, were notorious for their maintenance of segregated work roles. Sponsors could only be encouraged, not forced, to make provision for women in 'non-traditional' areas.[48]

Yet the problem was not just one of employers. Action research funded by the MSC found that MSC employees were also at fault. Staff would not accept, for instance, that girls could handle heavy weights in the building industry and thought that therefore to recruit them was to waste opportunities boys could profit from. A tutor only involved girls in a motor bike maintenance class by suggesting they upholstered the seat.[49]

The YOP scheme has now been replaced by the YTS, the Youth Training Scheme which became fully operational in September 1983. Whilst YOP was always seen as a programme to solve what was presented as a temporary problem, the new scheme is regarded by policy-makers as a step towards a permanent scheme for young people in general.

The scheme offers 12 months' work experience with occupationally relevant education through one of two Modes, Mode A and Mode B. In Mode A financial support is given to employers to train employed and unemployed young people. In Mode B there are schemes for unemployed young people through Training Workshops, Community Projects, Information Technology Centres (B1) and small employers (B2). Mode A schemes take by far larger numbers and girls made up about 44 per cent of those on the scheme at the end of 1983, and around 35 per cent of those in Mode B schemes at the same time. The acceptance by the MSC of many of the inadequacies of the YOP programme, including the recognition of the sex stereotyping that the programme mainly reinforced, led many to hope that the new scheme would be able to offer women[50] the opportunities YOP had denied them. However, all the signs suggest that exactly the same patterns are repeating themselves and that exactly the same excuses are being used. The use of Occupational Training Families (OTFs), for instance, to help structure the curriculum is thought to reinforce gender segregation. Career advisors, YTS managers and employers are thought not to encourage, and even on occasions discourage, any preferences by girls for 'non-traditional' areas of experience. The reliance of Mode A upon employers obviously raises the question again of how far it would be possible to impose changes on employers who cling to existing sex-stereotyping in their attitudes to employees.

The MSC continues to stress the importance of opening up new opportunities to women but there is little evidence to suggest that, as yet, the YTS is doing other than to perpetuate pre-existing stereotypes and divisions. There is even evidence of occasions when the MSC has appeared to be deliberately unwilling to countenance any expenditure on facilities like child care that are a necessity for many women attempting to take first steps outside the home and into the labour market.[51] The effective provision of training opportunities for women has to be seen as involving more than formal access to courses. Effective provision has to counter sexism within the courses and the paths into certain occupations but, as importantly, it has also to involve the provision of certain elements which recognize the demands placed on women by their existing dual role in the home. Flexibility of starting dates, compensatory pre-programmes in technical areas, childcare provision, advertising in the kinds of areas women frequent such as playgroups, health centres and supermarkets, all such elements should be seen as part of effective state training provision for women especially in the light of calls for on-going and recurrent training in the context of a changing labour market. Training is not just a matter for youth, but even where attention is focused on the school leaver substantial changes need to be effected to cope with the present patterns in training provision. These changes will require both internal re-education within the MSC and careful negotiation with employers. Such changes are not impossible if commitment rather than rhetoric is the keystone for MSC policy.

The importance of such a commitment in both policy *and* practice by the MSC is further illustrated by recent developments. In the not too distant past training and education were regarded as separate entities. In practice the distinction was not always so clear cut, but education was, in general, regarded as a more general preparation for life whilst training was felt to involve the provision of more explicitly technical skills that certain occupations required. Over the last decade and a half, in a context of rising youth unemployment, an economic recession and a tight labour market, a new vocationalism has developed in schools, a sense that schooling should prepare more directly for the labour market. One recent development has been the TVEI, the Technical and Vocational Education Initiative launched in 1983. In this initiative the MSC has poured funds into pilot projects in schools with the aim of producing more skilled youngsters, and equal opportunities was one of the main criteria the MSC expected LEAs (Local Education Authorities) to meet. Despite this, the structure of the pilot programmes appear to have been blatantly sex stereotyped in most cases.[52] Eagerness to get programmes set up combined with lack of effective equal opportunities criteria and efficient monitoring has resulted in a continuing gap between policy programmes and actual practice.

## CONCLUSION

Women are faced with patterns of representation which are male and therefore express male interests. There are few women in positions of authority in the government, in the MSC, amongst employers' federations or in the unions, yet these are precisely the groups mostly involved in policy decision-making in the area of training. When this situation changes then so will the prospects for women in general. Increasingly, analyses indict the way in which unions fail to represent their women members and conceptualize demands in terms of the interests of male members.[53] At the other extreme very few women have made it into high level managerial positions and their lack of promotion reflects very clearly a refusal by male managers to value women's work or open up opportunities.[54] If women did get into positions of authority a more general recognition of the abilities of women is likely to follow. However, to achieve this a programme of positive action and education appears necessary inside unions, inside the civil service, and inside business organizations. At the moment women are meeting obstacles at all levels and in a wide variety of sites. Without such changes it seems only too likely that the present pattern of limited opportunities for women and continued sex stereotyping will continue to exist. Organizations such as the MSC do not have the resources for evaluation and monitoring of their schemes even where a commitment to do better for women does exist at the top. It seems therefore that the focus of attention should be on the transformation of the practice of those on the ground in state training programmes so that they open up and welcome women in every area of work.

# NOTES AND REFERENCES

1. CSE Sex and Class Group, Mimeograph, 1981.
2. C. Cockburn, *Brothers*. London: Pluto Press, 1983, p. 113.
3. A. Phillips and B. Taylor (1980) Sex and skill: notes towards a feminist economics, *Feminist Review*, No. 6.
4. A. Pollert, *Girls, Wives, Factory Lives*, London: Macmillan, 1981, p. 65.
5. The number of centres fell from 23 in 1951 to 13 in 1962. However, by 1971 the numbers had increased to 1952. House of Commons Expenditure Committee, Seventh Report, London: HMSO, 1973.
6. Ministry of Labour, *Training for Skill: Recruitment and Training of Young Workers in Industry* (Carr Report), London: HMSO, 1958.
7. Ministry of Education, *15-18* (Crowther Report), London: HMSO, 1959.
8. Ministry of Education, *Half Our Future* (Newsom Report), London: HMSO, 1963.
9. Hilary Land, Sex role stereotyping in the social security and income tax systems, in J. Chetwynd and O. Hartnett (eds.), *The Sex Role System*, London: RKP, 1978; H. Land, Who cares for the family?, *The Journal of Social Policy*, July 1978; H. Land, The family wage, *Feminist Review*, No. 6, 1980. The male breadwinner family makes up 5 per cent of the present workforce. J. Coussins and A. Coote, *The Family in the Firing Line*, London: CPAG, 1981.
10. For example, in 1974 in CSE examinations 191,275 girls compared with 185,562 boys passed English; 59,482 girls passed in French compared with 37,127 boys. However, when it came to maths 142,801 girls passed compared to 152,672 boys; in physics the difference was even more notable—10,221 girls passed compared to 76,074 boys. The GCE results showed similar differences. See R. Deem, *Women and Schooling*, London: RKP, 1978, tables 3.2 and 3.3, pp. 67–68.
11. The Industrial Training Bill, 1964.
12. Frank Cousins of the Transport and General Workers Union is quoted to this effect in P. Perry, *The Evolution of British Manpower Policy*, London: Bacie, 1976, p. 106.
13. M. Woodhall, Investment in women: a reappraisal of the concept of human capital, *International Review of Education*, **19**, 1, 1973.
14. House of Commons Expenditure Committee, The Employment of Women, Sixth Report, London: HMSO, 1973. Evidence of the National Joint Committee of Working Women's Organizations, p. 84.
15. *Ibid.* Memorandum of the National Council of Women of Great Britain.
16. Dept. of Employment, Government Observations on three Reports on Youth Employment Services, the Employment of Women, and Employment Services and Training, Cmnd. 5536, London: HMSO, 1974.
17. House of Commons Expenditure Committee, *The Employment of Women*, Sixth Report, London: HMSO, 1973, p. 2106.
18. *Ibid.*
19. *Ibid.* Memorandum of the National Council of Women of Great Britain, p. 97.
20. Dept. of Employment, *Training for the Future—A Plan for Discussion*, London: HMSO, 1972.
21. Dept. of Employment, Employment and Training: Government Proposals, Cmnd. 5250, London: HMSO, 1973.
22. Dept. of Employment, Government Observations on Three Reports on Youth Employment Services, the Employment of Women and Employment Services and Training. CMND. 5536, London: HMSO, 1974.
23. MSC, Training Opportunities for Women, Training Services Agency, London: MSC, 1976.
24. Sex Discrimination Act, 1975.
25. Type of employment entered by school leavers in 1974:

| Class of employment | Boys % | Girls % |
|---|---|---|
| apprenticeship to a skilled occupation | 43.0 | 6.5 |
| employment leading to recognized professional qualifications | 1.3 | 1.7 |
| clerical employment | 7.0 | 40.5 |
| employment with planned training | 17.1 | 17.3 |
| other | 31.6 | 34.0 |

Source: Figure 4, *Training Opportunities for Women*, op. cit.

26. M. Alexander, *Equal Opportunities and Vocational Training*, Berlin: European Centre for the Development of Vocational Training, 1980, p. 9.
27. These statistics can be found in N. Fonda, Current entitlements and provisions: a critical review, in Fonda, N. and Moss, P. (eds.), *Mothers in Employments*, Middlesex: Brunel University, 1976, p. 43; S. Rothwell, United Kingdom, in Yohalem, A. (ed.), *Women Returning to Work*, London: Frances Pinter, 1980, p. 197; Alexander, op. cit., p. 9; Robarts, S., *Positive Action for Women*, London: NCCL, 1981, p. 87.
28. These have been the elements the EOC is most concerned about. See EOC, *Review of the Training Opportunities Scheme*, Manchester: EOC, 1978.
29. Alexander, op. cit., p. 9.
30. Fonda, op. cit.
31. Rothwell, op. cit.
32. S. Stoney and M. Reid, *Further Opportunities in Focus*, report of a project commissioned by the FEU from the National Foundation for Educational Research, 1980.
33. T. Keil and P. Newton, Into work—continuity and change, in Deem, R. (ed.), *Schooling for Women's Work*, London: RKP, 1980; Cook, A., Vocational training, the labour market and the unions, in Steinberg Ratner, R. (ed.), *Equal Employment Policy for Women*, Philadelphia: Temple University Press, 1980.
34. *Registered Unemployment*      1975      1980
    female          141,600      457,400
    male          650,200      1031,500
    that is a 59 per cent rise for men, a 223 per cent rise for women.
    EOC, *Submission of Written Evidence to the House of Lords Select Committee on Long-Term Remedies for Unemployment*, Manchester: EOC, 1980.
35. Some take a minimizing view of the possible impact of new technology, A. Sinfield, *What Unemployment Means*, London: Martin Robertson, 1981, p. 137. Others anticipate catastrophic effects. There appears to be no exact way of calculating the possible effects of technological change, L. Hesselman and R. Spellman Responses to the employment consequences of technological change, paper given to the Production Studies Group Conference on the Employment Consequences of Technological Change, September 1980. However, there is a consensus that it is areas of female employment that will be worst hit. J. Gershuny, Technical innovation and women's work in the EEC: a medium-term perspective, mimeograph, EEC Seminar on Women's Employment Prospects, Manchester, May 1980. E. Bird, *Information Technology in the Office: the impact on women's jobs*, Manchester: Equal Opportunities Commission, 1980.
36. J. Fawkes, Breaking the mould, *The Guardian*, 16 December 1981.
37. MSC, *Young People and Work* (Holland Report), London: MSC, 1977.
38. Between 1972 and 1977, the year of the report, the number of unemployed 16–17 year olds had risen 120 per cent compared to an overall rise of 45 per cent in unemployment.
39. MSC, *Young People and Work*, London: MSC, 1977, p. 7.
40. G. Holland, The Youth Opportunities Programme, *Trends in Education*, Summer 1979.
41. A typology of this new definition of skills is available in Schools Council Discussion Document, *Skills for Employment 1980*.
42. *TES*, 22 October 1976, 'What the PM said'.
43. After that three clear directions for future development emerged. The first dealt with vocational preparation for the employed. See DES, *A Better Start in Working Life*, Consultative Paper, London: HMSO, 1979. The second dealt with schools and work. See *Education in schools: a Consultative Document*, Cmnd. 6869, London: HMSO, 1977. The third dealt with the area of training. An overview of the latter two was provided in DES, *16–18, Education and Training for the 16–18 year olds: a Consultative Paper*, London: HMSO, 1978.
44. A major European Communities Action Programme was launched in 1976 by a resolution of Council and the Ministers of Education meeting in Council. It included pilot projects, reports on common themes, study visits and workshops, statistical guidelines and information arrangements. The European Social Fund has also been changed to provide assistance in this area.
45. MSC, *Opportunities for Girls and Women in the MSC Special Programmes for the Unemployed*, London: MSC, 1979.
46. MSC, *Annual Report 1978-9*, London: MSC, 1980.

47. MSC, *Review of the Second Year of Special Programmes*, London: MSC, 1980, p. 7.
48. S. Green, The employer's attitude to working mothers, in Fonda, N. and Moss, P. (eds.), *Mothers in Employment*, Middlesex: Brunel University, 1976. MSC, *Opportunities for Girls and Women in the MSC Special Programmes for the Unemployed*, London: MSC, 1979.
49. P. Brelsford et al., *Give Us a Break*, MSC Research and Development Series No. 11.
50. S. Davies, *Women and Training News*, No. 13, 1983.
51. Greenwich Employment Resource Unit, Skill Centre Report, 1984.
52. V. Millman, The new vocationalism, mimeograph, Girl Friendly Schooling Conference, 1984.
53. A. Phillips, *Hidden Hands*, London: Pluto Press, 1983.
54. R. Crompton and G. Jones, *White Collar Proletariat*, London: Macmillan, 1984.

# 7

# The Manpower Services Commission and the Youth Training Scheme:
## a permanent bridge to work?

### DAN FINN

As Britain has returned to levels of unemployment which many thought had
been left behind in the 1930s, we have, in common with many European
states, witnessed the creation of government programmes which have
attempted to ameliorate its worst effects. In the United Kingdom, the most
significant of these interventions have been those organized by the
Manpower Services Commission (MSC), a tripartite body which has
experienced a growth rate matched only by the increase in unemployment.

In place of a strategy of job creation, and apart from attempts to
manipulate the unemployment statistics, it is the programmes of the MSC
which represent the most *active* policies of the British government for
responding to the crisis of mass unemployment. Since its creation in 1974 its
activities have affected literally millions of people, kept thousands off the dole
queues, and structured the experiences of the vast majority of school-leavers
as they have made the hazardous transition to work or, increasingly, to
unemployment.

In the last five years these programmes, especially the youth programmes,
have had to go through various transformations to both retain political
support *and* accommodate the young unemployed. The initial response (the
Job Creation Programme), which defined unemployment as cyclical and the
problem as temporary, was designed for the most 'disadvantaged'. This was
followed by the Youth Opportunities Programme (YOP) in 1977 which by

Specially commissioned for this volume. © The Open University, 1985.

1982 had become the *only* source of work and income for many school-leavers.

In September 1983 YOP was replaced by the Youth Training Scheme (YTS), in which 460,000 places would be provided at a cost of about £1 billion. This programme guarantees the offer of a year's training, including 13 weeks off-the-job provision, to all minimum age school-leavers. It was anticipated that 300,000 trainees would be placed with employers in Mode A schemes. A further 160,000 trainees were to be accommodated in a more expensive mixture of local authority, state and voluntary provision, known as Mode B. At the same time, in an unprecedented bid to reshape and control elements of the curriculum in schools, the MSC launched the Technical and Vocational Education Initiative (TVEI) which has since been extended to cover every local education authority in the country.[1]

Remarkably the MSC has been able to cultivate extensive support for each phase of innovation and expansion. Despite reservations, a tripartite consensus between government, unions and employers has been carefully constructed around each new programme. However, far from it being the extension of a new democratic right of access to 'quality' training, I want to suggest that the YTS removes young people from the collective bargaining process and places them in a new twilight dependent status suspended midway between school and wage labour.

This process developed out of a critique of comprehensive schools which, by the late 1970s, were being held increasingly responsible for the inability of their pupils to obtain work. It was to remedy these 'failings' that YOP, and then the YTS and TVEI, were created. In contrast with the alleged irrelevance of 1960s educational reforms, the YTS in particular has been promoted as a new foundation training year which will act as a 'permanent bridge to work'. But how is it that schools were blamed for youth unemployment; and to what extent has the YTS been able to deliver the objectives that were set for it after YOP was replaced in 1983?

## YOUTH UNEMPLOYMENT AND COMPREHENSIVE EDUCATION

In the wake of the Callaghan-inspired Great Debate on Education,[2] initiated in 1976, it became a common assumption that comprehensive schools were failing to prepare their pupils for working life: that their curricula and teaching methods were irrelevant, if not positively antagonistic, to the demands of employers and the needs of the labour market. As the scale of youth unemployment escalated the employment problem of young people, their inability to get jobs came to be interpreted as an *educational* problem.

The causes of youth unemployment in this view, which was assiduously promoted in various reports and media, were comprehensive schools, progressive teaching methods, a liberal curriculum and examination reform. Young people were both educationally deficient and displayed a lack of willingness and poor attitudes to work. The perverse implication of this analysis was that in some way young people had actually chosen to be unemployed: they were the ones who were unwilling to accept the necessary disciplines and rigour of working life. Hence the subsequent emphasis on work experience to be added to the school timetable, for employers to be involved in schools, and for new examinations to be specifically vocational in character.

With well over three million unemployed, the fallacies in this argument are evident: even with 'appropriate' skills there are not enough jobs available for the young. The point is that youth unemployment was to be treated as an educational problem rather than an employment one for *political* reasons: the government cannot change the labour process and organization of work to fit existing school-leavers, but it could try to fit school-leavers to the existing priorities of employers. Thus, with school-leavers no longer receiving immediate work experience, schools and training programmes had to become the source of the work ethic. That is, under the new conditions the state was held responsible for the process of work socialization, a process that was previously a normal part of leaving school and getting a job.

The issue was not simply that of the usual role of schooling in the certification of labour, but the promotion of a concept of education as a *direct* preparation for work. Schooling for unemployment seems to require, quite paradoxically, more efficient education for employment: teachers, it seems, will now have to instil the work ethic deeply enough for it to survive lengthy periods of non-work.

It is in this context that we need to see both the TVEI and other vocational initiatives which are being introduced by the Department of Education and Science.[3] These innovations, and their funding, are imposing a new agenda on comprehensive schools. This 'new vocationalism' signals the abandonment of equal opportunity as the central reference point of educational strategy. The key element of these schemes is out-of-school work experience, and their guiding philosophy is to create an appropriate education for certain types of students, to be derived largely from their assumed destination in the division of labour.

These new programmes reduce the objectives of education to the provision of job-related skills. They have the effect of promoting and extending certain responses to the reality of youth unemployment, and the double effect of marginalizing and making more difficult other kinds of curricular responses. These vocational initiatives are cumulatively undermining some of the achievements of the comprehensive era; but as yet they have had nothing like the impact of the MSC's post-school training schemes. It is these programmes which have transformed both the experiences of school leavers and our perceptions of youth unemployment.

## YOUTH AND THE LABOUR PROCESS

Before moving on to evaluate the political structure and role of the MSC, it is important to consider briefly the relationship between youth and the labour market. Although, on a crude level, the expansion of training schemes may be interpreted as a means of 'laundering' the monthly unemployment statistics, it is necessary to grasp what those statistics are actually measuring; that is, a crisis of profitability to which employers have responded by the reorganization of the material conditions of production—by mass 'shake-outs' of labour, new investment and changes in the organization of work. Thus whilst employers themselves seem to believe that school-leavers are different from what they used to be, it is equally evident that there has been a change in the nature of labour demand.

Excluding a certain level of white collar work, state employment and some traditional apprenticeships, the juvenile labour market has historically been characterized by the large number of casual, dead-end occupations, for which employers have recruited school-leavers only to jettison them, without transferable skills, when they have become entitled to an adult wage. This has happened particularly in the distributive trades and certain sectors of manufacturing and clerical work. Indeed, the initial demand for day release education was advanced by the Labour movement precisely as a way of *protecting* young workers from such 'blind alley' employers.[4]

Since the war this casual labour market has suited many young men, who were having a 'fling' before settling down, and many young women, who saw their initial jobs as an interim between school and marriage. In conditions of full employment the focus of investigation and state policy was on providing 'rational' careers advice to counter the allegedly irrational work behaviour and job changes of school-leavers.[5] Young workers have always been characterized as casual, irresponsible, poorly motivated and quick to change jobs.

In the late 1970s what was new was the employers' expectation that school-leavers should have the sense of responsibility and commitment which are usually produced by work experience. This expectation was partly a result of the employers' power in a buyers' market; more fundamentally, it also reflected changes in the labour process, changes in the way that labour was used and controlled at work. Not only was there an absolute decline in the number of jobs available for school-leavers, but there was also a concomitant reorganization of the labour process in those jobs which remained. Simon Frith has argued that as a result of this transformation:

> Young workers today enter a labour market in which there are fewer and fewer openings for either skilled craftsmen or for unskilled casual labourers. The dominant demand is for generalized, semi-skilled labour power. The shifting employment opportunities resulting from the rise of service occupations, technological changes in production, the decline of small firms means, too, shifting modes of labour control. It is in this context that the young compete unequally with experienced adults. They lack commitment and discipline and

'realism'. These are the qualities which have to be instilled by the state, as it takes on responsibility for the now lengthy period of transition from school to work.[6]

The political response to youth unemployment, however, reflected more than their numbers. The extent and speed of state intervention was to signal the very real fears of the social unrest which could have been precipitated. Equally, it was also feared that a lengthy period of post-school unemployment would deny the exposure of the young to the work socialization, habituation and dependency which binds the mature, experienced worker to the labour process. In the 1970s these interventions were to be extensive and rapid, but their mobilization depended on more than mere administrative, financial or logistical considerations. They required a massive political and ideological realignment of the purposes and defined functions of education and training, an amplification of causes and promotion of explanations of the crisis, rather than a simple accommodation of its effects. If 'there was work to be done', as the MSC's first publication on this problem proclaimed,[7] that 'work' lay as firmly in the political and ideological terrain as it did in the application of technocratic procedures to the operation of the labour market.

## FROM YOP TO THE YTS

Although its ostensible remit was the reform of industrial training, the MSC has, since its creation, become one of the key state institutions acting to cool out and mitigate the social consequences of mass unemployment. As the recession decimated the apprenticeship system and caused the spectacular growth of youth unemployment, the problems about young people and work were increasingly circumscribed within a debate about education and training.

YOP was originally defined as an avenue into full-time work, but as this 'promise' soured with the arrival of two, then three, million unemployed, and as fewer trainees obtained jobs, so its credibility was steadily eroded. In its first year YOP affected one in eight school-leavers; by 1982 it was covering one in two; and in 1983 there were more school leavers on YOP courses than in normal jobs. In its five-year existence YOP provided temporary placements for nearly 1.9 million youngsters.

| Composition of YOP: 1978–83 | 1978/79 | 1979/80 | 1980/81 | 1981/82 | 1982/83 |
|---|---|---|---|---|---|
| Work experience (WEEP) | 128,200 | 182,100 | 304,500 | 461,500 | 393,400 |
| (% with private employers) | (84.5%) | (76.2%) | (79.5%) | (80.4%) | (78.6%) |
| Work preparation | 34,000 | 34,300 | 55,500 | 91,500 | 67,800 |
| Pilot YTS places (12 months long) | | | | | 81,900 |
| Total—All YOP | 162,200 | 216,400 | 360,000 | 553,000 | 543,100 |

The most contentious element of YOP concerned the large number of trainees placed with private employers, usually for six months. In 1981 Youthaid pointed out that they were 'concentrated in small, low-paying, non-unionized workplaces'.[8] Rather than philanthropic employers 'helping' the young unemployed, it became clear that many were using YOP to subsidize their recruitment procedures, if not directly exploiting young trainees as cheap labour.

As the programme expanded it became impossible to monitor and 'police' the scheme; vetting was perfunctory, and fewer on-site inspections were carried out. A growing proportion of youngsters were returned to unemployment at the end of their placements. Evidence accumulated that employers were substituting trainees for workers; the MSC admitted to a job substitution rate of at least 30 per cent. The government refused to increase the trainee allowance and its purchasing power fell steadily. Few trainees received off-the-job education or training; they were excluded from many aspects of employment legislation. Between 1980 and 1983 there were seventeen deaths and over 9000 injuries to trainees. There were also many complaints about the arbitrary discipline procedures being imposed by employers.[9]

In place of a scheme intended to improve the employment prospects of the young, and get them into work, a pool of vulnerable cheap labour was created. At best YOP was redistributing unemployment; it was doing nothing to reduce it. By 1981 there was a groundswell of opposition and the first indications that young people were refusing to take up places. Unions became disenchanted: Tower Hamlets Trades Council argued that 'every major promise that was given by the MSC to the trade union movement has been broken, ignored and manipulated'.[10] Motions were submitted to the annual Trades Union Congress calling for a withdrawal of union co-operation. Congress accepted many of the arguments, but the particular resolutions were eclipsed in a new debate initiated by the MSC, which appeared to secure both the long-standing TUC policy of day-release education for young workers and a new right of access to 'quality' training for unemployed school-leavers. The abuses of YOP were admitted, but the focus of attention shifted. After a consultative process, the MSC, voluntary organizations, employers and many trade union officials were to launch a concerted campaign to win support for a new training programme—the YTS.


## THE TUC AND THE MSC

To explain how the TUC and many individual unions endorsed these new proposals, we should understand how they had initially become enmeshed with the MSC. Since the last war, the trade union movement has called for government intervention to impose coherence on the chaotic training arrangements that characterize many sectors of employment. At the same time, the TUC has become involved in a range of corporate organizations which have attempted, with varying degrees of success, to modernize the British economy.

The high point of this process was the period of the 'social contract' initiated by the 1974/79 Labour government. In return for wage restraint and a curb on militancy, the TUC and its affiliates were offered legislative concessions and a more direct involvement in the management of the economy. It was in this context that, in 1974, the MSC came into existence.

The MSC's constitution guaranteed union representation and in contrast to earlier arrangements was empowered to pursue more vigorous policies for the reform of industrial training. The trade union movement saw within this a major advance, which seemed to be confirmed when the Labour government expanded the direct training services of the MSC, became more heavily involved in supporting the recession-hit apprenticeship system and developed special programmes for the unemployed.

The first Thatcher government was, however, determined to reverse state involvement in these areas, and the budget of the MSC was slashed. The Conservatives proposed to return training to market forces. In opposing these policy changes, the TUC became more committed, arguing for the MSC's expansion in response to accelerating unemployment.

In the wake of the inner-city riots of 1981, which were partly blamed on unemployment, the Tories were converted; they did a 'U-turn', and expanded provision for the young. Paradoxically, this took place at the same time that individual trade unions were being ousted from other MSC bodies. In particular, seventeen Industrial Training Boards, which had imposed some coherence on patterns of training, were abolished.[11]


## THE STRATEGIC IMPORTANCE OF THE MSC

The MSC has been concerned to create new forms of local involvement in dealing with the unemployed. It established a structure of area boards composed of nominees from the TUC, employers and the voluntary sector. These boards are responsible for approving schemes. They have enabled the MSC to present itself as open and democratic, when it has actually bypassed established democratic and collective bargaining procedures. Thus local authorities have little formal involvement, and can only compete for MSC resources on the same grounds as other sponsors; while many trade union officials and lay members have approved schemes without reference to criteria (for instance, rate of pay, job security, discipline, and so on) which they would normally apply in collective bargaining.

Though area boards have formal authority over the scheme, the reality is more complex. In effect, the boards obscure the way in which real operational power remains firmly entrenched in the hands of the civil service which controls the collection and presentation of data, the monitoring of schemes, the allocation of resources and the construction of policy. The MSC has developed into a tightly structured bureaucracy with massive administrative power.

Colin Ball, one of the civil servants involved in the creation of YOP, has described another way in which the MSC exercises this control. He points to a key element in MSC practice, the protection of their central authority by the division of operational responsibility amongst a host of sponsors.[12] Ideologically, because this involves community groups, employers, local authorities, colleges and voluntary organizations, the MSC is able to present itself as involving the whole of the community. In reality, he witnessed a process of divide and rule, where few sponsors could challenge the entrenched power of the bureaucracy.

The MSC has not, therefore, been a simple palliative. It represents a bureaucratic response to the political problems posed by unemployment. It focuses attention, not on the crisis of production and investment, but on the qualities and capacities of the workforce. It takes for granted the demands of employers and seeks to adjust the supply of labour accordingly. The MSC is not engaged in combating class, sexual and racial privilege: its activities have simply reproduced and reinforced these basic distinctions. Only by grasping these broader points can one appreciate why the MSC has been given such massive resources; and why it is now proposed that they should control up to a quarter of all non-advanced further education.[13]

Although initially hostile to special programmes for the unemployed, the Thatcher government soon came to appreciate their strategic importance. In their battles over rates and public expenditure, the MSC offered a route for bypassing the political control of local authorities, who might have put those resources to other uses, such as extending conventional educational opportunities. The MSC was also successful in implementing low-wage Conservative proposals which under other circumstances would have been vigorously opposed. Crucially though, the MSC has transformed the experiences of most school-leavers and has profoundly affected the ways in which we can think about unemployment.

## TRAINING WITHOUT JOBS

From its inception the MSC helped to evolve the mythology that youth unemployment was caused by a 'mismatch' between young workers' capacities and the characteristics required by employers. They formally acknowledged the economic factors underlying the growth of unemployment, but it was the notion of mismatch which ideologically informed the internal development of their programmes.

At the same time as it obscured the structural nature and causes of youth unemployment, the notion of mismatch facilitated the attainment of other objectives. In the first place, smothered in a rhetoric of concern, it enabled young people to be taken off the streets into workplaces and colleges, into a 'safe' environment, thereby demonstrating that the state was doing something to tackle unemployment. Secondly, the ideology of mismatch firmly located the problem within the unemployed themselves. The almost total focus on the labour market, and on job-finding and job-keeping, reinforced the myth that there were appropriate jobs available to anyone who had the 'social skills' and persistence to find and secure them; a set of ideas which conveniently deflected attention from the structural problems of British capitalism. Finally, the crisis of youth unemployment and the related employers' critique of educational standards created the political and ideological space which facilitated new forms of state intervention in training and education.

In addition the MSC also had a transformative role. It created training programmes and courses, and developed specific forms of work induction, which were not solely concerned with the transmission of objective skills. These, too, had their hidden curriculum conveying meanings about the nature of wage labour and skills, and about the status and expectations of youngsters. As part of its wider objectives, the MSC was involved in transforming the cultural meanings and definitions of the young.

The period between 1978 and 1982 was marked by a working out in practice of new definitions of the rights, opportunities and possibilities for those young people who, despite mass unemployment, still choose to leave school at the earliest possible moment. Under the leadership of the MSC, and in the form of YOP, new structural relationships between education, training, employers and young people were explored and created. Internally, a new vocabulary of vocational preparation and generic skills was to evolve within these programmes, which presented themselves as meeting the needs of the young unemployed but which, in fact, defined the young as in need of new forms of provision. In this redefinition of 'youth', young workers were to be effectively separated from the political question of full employment.

By 1982 the opening paragraph of the document on which the YTS is based was able to argue, as if it were a virtue, that 'This report is about providing a permanent bridge between school and work. It is not about youth unemployment'.[14] From the early days of MSC interventions, with their ostensible emphasis on job creation and getting the unemployed into work, we have witnessed the creation of a programme which is solely focused on the training and employability of young school-leavers. The YTS has been released from *any* obligation actually to place the young in jobs.

Young school-leavers, then, are not just accidental victims of the recession. Rather, having been excluded from the labour market, they are now being actively redefined as trainees, as an aspect of the state's solution to the recession.

## THE YOUTH TRAINING SCHEME: THE FIRST YEAR

The government and the MSC have claimed a large measure of success for the first year of YTS. They point to the 450,000 training places created and the participation of many school-leavers, and dismiss their critics as misguided or malevolent. Government ministers have claimed that most trainees have obtained jobs, and that they are well on the way towards providing a foundation training which will act as a permanent bridge to work.

We should be wary, however, of accepting this 'success' at face value. There is considerable evidence to suggest that the YTS has, in practice, become something very different from the wonderful new opportunity described by MSC rhetoric.

In the first place, it is important to remember that the YTS was no simple creation of the Conservative government. When it considered replacing the much-criticized and disliked YOP, the Thatcher administration, in a White Paper published in 1981, proposed the introduction of a one-year traineeship for all unemployed school-leavers, who would be paid £15 a week and would lose their entitlement to supplementary benefit.

This provoked considerable hostility: the Careers Service, voluntary organizations, FE lecturers and some employers were hostile to a programme which would virtually conscript the young unemployed into low paid traineeships, and the TUC stated unequivocally that they would not support the scheme unless there was a higher allowance and no compulsion. As a result the MSC, which had initiated the debate, set up a tripartite working party to produce a more acceptable set of proposals.

The Youth Task Group, made up of employer, trade union and government representatives, came forward with their alternative proposals in April 1982. They suggested a comprehensive training scheme embracing employed and unemployed 16-year-olds, paying £25 a week. It was to be a 'quality' scheme, and participation would be voluntary. Their recommendations were grudgingly accepted by Norman Tebbit, then Employment Secretary.

The YTS was able to attract public support in an election year because of the claimed removal of the abuses of YOP and the offer of 'quality' training to unemployed school-leavers. More important perhaps, was the ubiquitous offer of a job conjured up by publicity which described the YTS as a permanent bridge to work, and attempted to associate it with the new technologies at the forefront of employment creation.

In reality, however, developments in the first year have seen an abandonment of those election year pretensions, and the reduction of YTS to a mechanism for producing the workforce that the government thinks is appropriate to the depressed circumstances of the late 1980s.

In contrast with the trainee-centred focus of the Youth Task Group Report, the last two years has been characterized by the promotion of YTS as an employer-led scheme. This has not simply reflected the need to secure training places, but has indicated a considerable change in emphasis; signalled by a series of concessions to employers.

Employers have retained complete control over hiring and firing trainees, and, where they use colleges, have been granted special discounts on charges for off-the-job educational provision. Trainees are excluded from Employment Protection, from most of the Race and Sex Discrimination Acts, and Health and Safety provision is inadequate.[15] Arrangements for monitoring employers are even less effective than they were under YOP, and there is virtually no mechanism for ensuring that trainees do not displace employees. MSC officials have explicitly encouraged employers to transform their young employees or apprentices into trainees.

Racial and sexual divisions are already emerging between the different modes and types of provision.[16] An analysis of just under 25,000 YTS 'start' certificates revealed that youngsters from ethnic minority backgrounds were 'less likely to be found in Mode A places' or 'have employee status'. It was found that 65 per cent of girls were being trained in administrative, clerical and sales areas, compared with 16 per cent of the boys; and 45 per cent of boys were in the maintenance, repair and manufacturing areas, compared with 7 per cent of girls.

Schemes negotiated nationally by the Large Companies Unit (a division of the MSC), which account for a third of the places offered by employers, are not subject to the approval or limited scrutiny of Area Manpower Boards.

More disturbingly, many of the local employer-based places are organized by private training agencies. These are entrepreneurial organizations which the MSC will largely entrust to monitor themselves. In Birmingham, where over half the places are controlled by such agencies, the local NATFHE branch has already established that many of them have questionable credentials.[17] Local monitoring projects in Manchester and London have found that 37 and 25 per cent respectively of locally approved Mode A places are organized by private training agencies.

Alongside these private agencies it appears that local Mode A provision is dominated by employer-based training organizations and consortia. Few local employers are directly involved, and it seems that the YTS has been unsuccessful in absorbing many young workers: the number of employed trainees anticipated on the scheme has been revised downwards from an original one third of the total to some 5 per cent. It seems that some conventional employment is being directly displaced by the YTS, but more critically, that many employers are less than enthusiastic about introducing a training programme for their young workers.

The new managing agencies that dominate YTS provision are the vehicle through which YOP Mark II is being created. In place of the quality training of large and medium-sized firms which was promised, many trainees are again being placed in small, non-unionized, low-paying workplaces. There are 4200 Mode A managing agents using over 100,000 different workplaces. In Cheshire, sixteen managing agents who were given approval to provide 2500 places are sub-contracting the trainee's work experience to over 1300 placements; all but a few dozen of which are the same small shops and businesses that were involved in YOP.

With respect to quality, there have been many complaints about the irrelevance of much of the off-the-job provision. An HMI survey of courses for YTS trainees in further education colleges complained about the lack of integration between the youngsters' work experience and their vocational studies, and reported 'many instances of teaching and learning taking place in depressing conditions that failed to provide adequate practical working environments'. They also pointed out that the poor educational achievements of many of the trainees were hardly likely to be improved by 'the 40–50 teaching hours usually allocated to these subjects'.[18]

More importantly, the on-the-job training—which is the most significant element of the scheme—is not assessed; and it is legitimate to question the MSC's capacity to enforce standards in a scheme which has no effective monitoring or skill testing. Unlike our European competitors, the YTS will simply provide trainees with a certificate which, without testing of standards, must be of questionable value.

The MSC suggests that it is creating a work-based alternative to conventional educational qualifications.[19] However, the wider educational claims of the MSC were shattered when they issued early guidelines for the off-the-job provision which specifically excluded considering matters 'relating to the organisation and functioning of society in general'. Young people, it seemed, could learn how to fill in application forms, but could not discuss why they were unemployed. Although those particular guidelines were toned-down, the Employment Minister responsible—Peter Morrison—had revealed his understanding of the scheme in a Commons Debate in July 1983:

> The scheme is not a social service. Its purpose is to teach youngsters what the real world of work is all about. That means arriving on time, giving of their best during the working day, and perhaps staying on a little longer to complete an unfinished task.

Such sentiments expressed by government ministers, alongside proclamations from the chairman of the MSC, suggest that this programme is more concerned with providing employers with a pool of cheap and vulnerable labour, from which they can pick and choose their recruits, than it has to do with meeting the training and educational needs of the young unemployed.

The first year of the YTS has been marked by a gradual transition from the consensual objectives originally outlined, towards a much closer subordination to the government's overall strategy. In essence, this involves using the YTS as part of an attack on the financial autonomy of local authorities; the privatization of public services; 'freeing' employers from legislative constraints; marginalizing trade union involvement; undermining comprehensive education; and 'pricing' the young back into work.[20]

Because of a lower than expected participation rate, the government reduced the number of approved YTS places for 1984/85 to 413,000; a reduction of some 7 per cent. But within this total, Mode A employer-based provision was increased by some 2500 places, whereas Mode B provision was cut by some 20 per cent. The impact of these reductions largely fell on trainee-centred, community-based agencies. The first year of YTS was punctuated by public controversy as established voluntary agencies were subjected to widespread disruption and cutbacks almost irrespective of the quality of their training. This was justified by reference to the abundance of employer-based places, but in reality was precipitated because school leavers responded to their new 'opportunity' with considerable ambivalence.

## THE REACTIONS OF SCHOOL LEAVERS

At the end of May 1984 over 375,000 young people had entered the YTS, but only 238,000 of these were still attending; occupying less than 60 per cent of available places. Of the 137,000, or 37 per cent of cumulative entrants unaccounted for, the MSC admitted that it did not know how many had left, where they had gone, or how many had been counted twice because they moved from one training place to another. As many as a third had probably gone straight back to the dole. Whatever the explanation, there is clear evidence that a substantial number of school leavers have been unwilling to become involved in YTS; and that many trainees have left the programme before completion.

This has taken place in a context where Job Centres have resorted to sending threatening letters to unemployed school leavers, and where, by the end of June, over 10,000 young people had had their benefit cut for leaving the scheme early or for refusing to take up a place. In less than a year, a voluntary 'quality' training scheme was beginning to look like a compulsory dose of work experience. Indeed, in December 1984, in a Christmas present to future unemployed school leavers, Margaret Thatcher announced that her government would be taking steps to remove their right to supplementary benefit as 'young people ought not to be idle', and 'should not have the option of being unemployed'.

Yet the lack of enthusiasm for the YTS displayed by many school leavers has not been the product of fecklessness, irresponsibility or idleness. Despite the seductive images of MSC publicity, there are enormous variations within the YTS. Some employers offer good training, with a chance of a job at the end, but other sponsors clearly offer what many school-leavers see as an extension of YOP, and experience as a spell of cheap labour. Crucially, the persistence of mass youth unemployment is undermining the YTS. Although government representatives, such as the Chancellor of the Exchequer, have claimed that 'about 70 per cent of youngsters leaving the scheme have gone *straight* into work or further training', the evidence so far produced by the MSC has merely shown that 56 per cent of a small sample of ex-trainees were in full-time work. Apart from those actively involved in part-time work, education or training, the survey showed that 34 per cent were unemployed and a further 7 per cent 'intended' to enter education or training. The pressure group, Youthaid, publicly complained about the 'seriously misleading information' given to Parliament about the job prospects of YTS leavers.[21]

Trainees are now entering a depressed labour market where their job prospects are being squeezed by competition from experienced adults and a new batch of subsidized school leavers. After those aged over 50, under 25-year-olds are more vulnerable to prolonged unemployment than any other group.

In October 1984 Youthaid estimated that half of the country's under-18s and one in four of the under-25s were out of work. Over half a million under-25-year-olds had been unemployed for more than six months, and more than 330,000 of them had been continuously unemployed for more than a year. There were over 270,000 unemployed youngsters aged 18 and over who had *never* had a full-time job since leaving school. Many of this generation of young workers are being consigned to the margins of the economy, to alternate between badly paid jobs and spells of unemployment. These realities are having serious implications for the credibility of the YTS and for the reactions of young people to it. The YTS is being experienced as much as a 'gangplank to the dole' as it is as a 'permanent bridge to work'.

## NOTES AND REFERENCES

1. On the launching of TVEI, see the article by Dale in this volume. Many of the educational issues have been debated in the pages of *Forum*, 25, 3, and 26, 1 and 2.
2. For an extended discussion of the politics of education in this period see Education Group, Centre for Contemporary Cultural Studies (1981) *Unpopular Education: Schooling and Social Democracy since 1944*, Hutchinson, London, chapters 9 and 10.
3. Many of these developments are assessed by Geoff Esland and Heather Cathcart in The compliant creative workers: the ideological reconstruction of the school leaver, Paper No. 84/22e, *Proceedings of the Standing Conference on the Sociology of Further Education*, Blagdon, Coombe Lodge.
4. For a contemporary account of the 'blind alley' debate in the 1930s, see Gollan, J., *Youth Into British Industry*, (1937) Left Book Club, Victor Gollancz, London. For a more recent assessment of the debate, see the article by G. and T. Rees, Juvenile unemployment and the state between the wars, in Rees, T. and Atkinson, P. (eds.), (1982) *Youth Unemployment and State Intervention*, Routledge & Kegan Paul, London.

5. See, for example, M. Carter (1966) *Into Work*, Pelican Books, Harmondsworth.
6. S. Frith, *Education, Training and the Labour Process*, unpublished paper given to the CSE Education Group, Birmingham University, November 1977, p. 4.
7. S. Mukherjee (1974) *There's Work to be Done: Unemployment and Manpower Policies*, MSC/HMSO, London.
8. Youthaid (1981) *Quality or Collapse? Youthaid Review of the Youth Opportunities Programme*, p. 4. Available from 9 Poland Street, London, W1.
9. For detailed evidence on these points see the report from Sheffield Trades Council (April, 1982) *A Trade Union Response to YOPs and NTI*, YOP Working Party, c/o 18 Parkhead Crescent, Sheffield, S11 9RD. Alternatively, see the report produced by D. Carter and I. Stewart (TGWU Officers in Manchester) (1982) *YOP, Youth Training and the MSC: The need for new Trade Union response*, available from Manchester Employment Research Group, 300 Oxford Road, Manchester M13.
10. Tower Hamlets Trades Council (1981) *Opportunity Knocks? Youth Unemployment and the Youth Opportunities Programme: A Discussion Paper for Trade Unionists*, p. 11. Available from 196 Cable Street, London, E1.
11. For an excellent appraisal and critique of overall government policy on industrial training, and a description of the dismantling of the Industrial Training Boards, see Greater London Training Board (1983) *The Youth Training Scheme in London*, GLC, London.
12. Colin Ball, Here comes Super YOP, *New Society*, 20 August 1981.
13. Currently the MSC accounts for about £90m of the estimated £800m of work-related non-advanced further education in England and Wales. A White Paper, *Training for Jobs*, proposed to increase the MSC share to £155m in 1985/86, and to £200m (about 25 per cent) in 1986/87, with corresponding reductions in local authority expenditure (Cmnd 9135, paragraph 46, February 1984). This aspect of the White Paper has been widely criticized. The Association of Metropolitan Authorities have argued:

> This MSC take-over will add to bureaucracy. It will not add a penny to the money spent on training. It will not create jobs. But, it could well lead to decreasing standards of education, to second-rate training and to a diversion of funds and training opportunities away from areas of high unemployment to areas where unemployment is relatively low.

14. Manpower Services Commission (April, 1982) *Youth Task Group Report*, MSC, London, para 1.1.
15. See, for example, Q. McDermott, Dying for a job, *New Statesmen*, 27 July 1984; or article on Safety on YTS, *Labour Research*, December 1984.
16. See, for example, the report from the Commission for Racial Equality (October, 1984) *Racial Equality and the Youth Training Scheme*, CRE, Elliot House, 10/12 Allington Street, London, SW1.
17. NATFHE, Birmingham Liaison Committee (January, 1984) *The Great Training Robbery: An Interim Report on the Role of Private Training Agencies within the YTS in Birmingham and Solihull*, Birmingham TURC, 7 Frederick Street, Birmingham 1. See also the article exposing the activities of Computotech Ltd, a private training agency heavily involved in MSC programmes, also entitled 'The Great Training Robbery', *Private Eye*, 14 December 1984.
18. Department of Education and Science (1984) *The Youth Training Scheme in Further Education 1983–84; An HMI Survey*, see pp. 11, 21 and 9.
19. 'MSC sets out skills list', *Times Educational Supplement*, 25 May 1984.
20. The only other programme directed specifically at the young unemployed is the Young Workers Subsidy, covering 130,000 young people. This scheme deliberately invites employers to pay below the rates of pay established by collective bargaining and Wages Councils. From this Autumn the scheme will be restricted to 17 year olds. Employers will receive a £15 a week subsidy if they pay *below* £50 a week. There is a suggestion that in the future only YTS graduates will be eligible for YWS. The pattern which the government is offering many school-leavers is therefore: £25 per week under YTS at 16, followed by £50 or less under YWS at 17.
21. See the argument reported in *Youthaid Bulletin*, No. 19, December 1984.

# Index